COMMUNICATION
Across Contexts
A Listening-Centered Approach

EYES

EARS

UNDIVIDED ATTENTION

HEART

Mary Lahman • Michelle Calka • Judd Case
Manchester University

Kendall Hunt
publishing company

Cover image © Shutterstock, Inc.

The Chinese symbol for "to listen" on the front cover reminds us that to listen effectively, we must use our ears, eyes, and heart while we give our full attention.

Kendall Hunt
publishing company

www.kendallhunt.com
Send all inquiries to:
4050 Westmark Drive
Dubuque, IA 52004-1840

Copyright © 2014 by Kendall Hunt Publishing Company

ISBN 978-1-4652-4988-3

All rights reserved. No part of this publication may be reproduced, stored in a retrieval system, or transmitted, in any form or by any means, electronic, mechanical, photocopying, recording, or otherwise, without the prior written permission of the copyright owner.

Printed in the United States of America

TABLE OF CONTENTS

CHAPTER 1 **Human Communication** 1

    Why Take a Course in Human Communication? 1

    What is Communication Competence? 2
        Assumptions about Communication 2
        Communication Competence: Components and Levels 3
        Communication Competence Grid 4

    How Does *Motivation* Build Communication Competence? 5
        Personality Style and Motivation to Communicate 6
        Listening is Ethical 6

    What *Knowledge* Builds Communication Competence? 7

    What *Skills* Build Communication Competence? 11
        Listening Choices Involved in an Ethics of Listening 11
        Listening Purposes and Contexts 12

CHAPTER 2 **Public Communication** 15

    What Responsibilities Do Communicators Have in Public Communication Contexts? 15

    As a Speaker, How Do I Discover Which Ideas to Present? 16
        Audience and Situational Analysis 17
        Rhetoric and the Rhetorical Canons 18

    As a Speaker, How Do I Use *Invention*? 18
        Reasoning 19
        Deductive vs. Inductive Logic 19
        Forms of Reasoning 20
            Argument by Definition 20
            Argument by Sign 20

Argument by Cause..21
Argument by Generalization................................21
Argument by Analogy..21
Logical Fallacies..22
Cause-effect..22
Generalization..22
Fallacies of irrelevance..23
Supporting Material..23

As a Speaker, How Do I Use *Arrangement* (Organization)?....................25
Speech Plan..26

As a Speaker, How Do I Use *Style* (Language)?.........................27
Concrete Language..28
Figurative Language..29

As a Speaker, How Do I Use *Delivery* (Nonverbal Cues) and *Memory*?..........................30
Physical Delivery..30
Vocal Delivery..31
Memory..32
Speech Criticism..32

As a Listener, How Do I Sustain an Ethics of Listening?......................33
Listening Behaviors..33

CHAPTER 3 Interpersonal Communication 37

What Communication Skills Transfer from Public to Interpersonal Communication Settings?........................37

How Do Listening, Language, and Nonverbal Communication Work Together to Build Supportive Communication Climates?......38
Supportive Communication Climates....................38
Description versus Evaluation................................38
Problem Orientation versus Control....................40
Spontaneity versus Strategy..................................40
Empathy versus Neutrality......................................40
Equality versus Superiority....................................41
Provisionalism versus Certainty............................41
Listening and Supportive Climates......................43
Nonverbal Cues across Cultures..........................43

What Interpersonal Skills Will Help Transform Interpersonal Conflict?..45

Attentiveness 45
Coordination 46
Composure 46
Expressiveness 47

CHAPTER 4 **Small Group Communication 49**

What Do You Like About Working in Small Groups? 49
    Key Characteristics of a Small Group 50
        Group Size 50
        Interdependence 50
        Shared Identity and Norms 51

What Skills Will Be Helpful in Managing Group Meetings? 52
    Group Roles 53
        Task Roles 53
        Relational Roles 53
        Ego-Centered Roles 54
    Managing Group Meetings 54
        Agendas 55
        Minutes 56

How Do Groups Make Good Decisions? 57
    The Standard Agenda for Decision Making 57
    Appreciative Inquiry as a Means of Organizational Change 58
    Challenges to Group Decision Making 59
        Grouphate 59
        Groupthink 59
    Preventing Groupthink 60

What Leadership Skills do You Have?
Which Ones do You Want to Develop? 61
    Becoming a Leader 61
    Leadership Styles 62

How Have You Resolved Group Conflict? 62
    Types of Group Conflict 63
    Conflict Management Styles 63

How Do Listening, Language, and Nonverbal Behaviors
Work Together in Small Group Communication? 65

Glossary **69**

CHAPTER 1

HUMAN COMMUNICATION

LEARNING OBJECTIVES

By the end of this chapter, you should be able to:

- Recognize the assumptions about communication and why they are inaccurate.
- Explain the components and levels involved in communication competence.
- Use the four areas of the competence grid to evaluate your communication competence.
- Describe how the information transfer, SMCR (source, message, channel, and receiver), and transactional models contribute to an understanding of the communication process.
- Explain the choices involved in an ethics of listening.

WHY TAKE A COURSE IN HUMAN COMMUNICATION?

To complete a degree? To become a good friend? To find a job? To be promoted? Because many students take a course in human communication to fulfill a requirement, communication instructors often use these appeals to gain attention. Some authors highlight miscommunication with friends and family members, or reveal startling statistics about the need for effective communication skills to find and keep a job. Other writers immediately delve into how communication works, ignoring the individual "student" within the "university student audience." What motivates you to read textbooks? Fear of a pop quiz? Curiosity about subject matter?

We hope that you will be motivated to study human communication to become a "person of ability and conviction who draws upon education and faith to lead a principled, productive, and compassionate life that improves the human condition" (see Manchester University, North Manchester, 2013, para. 1). Because we define **human communication** as *human meaning making,* we explore how communication is a dynamic process that involves people adapting to various **cultures** (*the values and behaviors shared by a group*) and **contexts** (*public speaking, interpersonal, and small group settings*), thus improving the human condition.

Consequently, we arranged this book to build **communication competence**—the ability to choose behaviors that are both appropriate and effective for a given context (Spitzberg & Cupach, 1984). In Chapter 2, we explore what it means to be effective and appropriate producers and consumers of messages in a public speaking context—persuasive speaking. In Chapters 3 and 4, we explore skills needed to communicate more competently in interpersonal and small group contexts.

We begin this chapter by discussing what you know about communication from your personal and educational experiences. We explore what we know about communicating appropriately and effectively.

WHAT IS COMMUNICATION COMPETENCE?

What is communication competence? How can people communicate appropriately and effectively? We answer these questions and more in the section that follows.

Assumptions about Communication

Begin by taking the following "communication background test." As you do so, think about a recent interaction with a friend:

1.	T	F	Words have meaning.
2.	T	F	Communication is a verbal process.
3.	T	F	Telling is communicating.
4.	T	F	Communication competence equals effectiveness.

(adapted from McCroskey, Richmond, & McCroskey, 2006, p. 16)

Once you determine whether the statements are true *or* false, continue reading to understand how *all* of the statements are false.

Many contend that Statement 1 is true because dictionaries provide meanings of words. We soon discover, however, how *meaning* is in people, not in the **language**—symbols used to negotiate meaning—they use. As we prepare persuasive presentations and transform interpersonal relationships, we learn that the meanings we intend may not be the meanings people attribute to our language choices.

Some recognize that Statement 2 is false because human communication is not *just* a verbal process; we are well aware of how much hand gestures, facial expressions, and other such behaviors communicate to others. Hence, we explore a number of ***nonverbal codes***—cues that stand alone or accompany languages, such as personal space, time, silence, and clothing—and discover the importance of these codes as we communicate across contexts and cultures.

Students of any age find daily evidence that Statement 3 is false. Telling is *not* communicating because merely hearing information may not result in understanding the material being presented; meaning making involves communicators listening *and* speaking. For example, a professor may tell you about a concept during a lecture, but if you do not pay attention or do not understand, you are not receiving the message. Communicators must involve each other by tying new concepts to familiar ones. Listeners must find relevance in messages to avoid turning a deaf ear. Speakers need to choose words that resonate with listeners. Each communicator benefits from a ***listening-centered approach***, where we seek first to understand the perspective of the other person.

Finally, because communication competence is not based solely on effectiveness, Statement 4 is false. For example, we can be effective when we interrupt another person because we get the chance to share our thought, but we are behaving inappropriately by not letting the other person finish his or her thoughts. Competent communicators must demonstrate both appropriate *and* effective behaviors across contexts and cultures. We can be effective, but not appropriate, and therefore not demonstrate communication competence.

Communication Competence: Components and Levels

Spitzberg and Cupach (1984) detailed three components needed for humans to be competent communicators: ***motivation*** (the desire to communicate), ***knowledge*** (understanding how to communicate), and ***skills*** (demonstrating effective and appropriate behaviors).

We can also think about communication competence as having two levels. On the surface level, we are expected to behave in socially appropriate and effective ways, which is called ***performative competence***. On a deeper level, we need to have the knowledge to perform competently, which is called ***process competence***, and involves all of the knowledge and cognitive activity to create the performance (Trenholm & Jensen, 2013).

We can have one level of competence without the other. Imagine attending a church service for a religion with which you are unfamiliar. You may pick up on the socially acceptable ways to act in this specific context, but you may not have the process competence to understand why these behaviors are performed. Likewise, you might have the process competence to act appropriately and effectively in a situation, but you do not actually behave that way. All that others see is the surface-level action. It is important to know not just *how* to be appropriate and effective but to be able to read the situation well enough to know *why*.

Because work places and living spaces need people who articulate and listen to reasoned arguments, transform conflicts, and complete small group tasks, understanding these key misconceptions about communication should change the way that we interact with others. Paying close attention to words and gestures, in addition to asking clarifying questions, maximizes interpersonal effectiveness. We become competent communicators when we learn appropriate *and* effective communicative behaviors.

For example, a competent communicator knows what to say and do based on the cultural rules and norms of a specific context. For example, students in the United States raise their hands before asking questions in a classroom, but these same students would find this behavior humorous if they raised their hands to be recognized when eating lunch with a group of friends. Hence, we change behavior based on context and culture.

If the language and nonverbal behaviors that you exhibit follow the rules and norms of an ethical context, your communication is considered ***appropriate***. Consequently, appropriateness is determined based on what others perceive as suitable in a given context (Spitzberg, 1983). For example, consider what constitutes appropriate communication when you hang out with a group of close friends. Do you communicate the same way with your grandparents? What about in the classroom? Your language choices, jokes, and demeanor are probably different in each situation, because appropriateness is determined by what others deem appropriate in that context.

> **CELL PHONES AND COMMUNICATION COMPETENCE**
>
> Cell phones create communication contexts and make demands of our performative and process competence. If we are appropriate and effective, we can use them to strengthen our relationships, manage our schedules, and illustrate our conversations. Have you used your cell phone to coordinate a study group or work group? To watch a video for class? To check in with a roommate or family member? To show pictures you took while studying abroad? If you have, then you may have used it to meet your goals (and with aplomb).
>
> However, cell phones can sometimes create contexts that we can't quite manage. We can be caught between attending to our phones and to the people around us. Our phones can interrupt study, contribute to misunderstandings, and sound-off during class. As cell phone researcher Richard Ling wrote in his book *New Tech, New Ties*, cell phones can "result in awkward co-present situations," but they can also "support better contact within the personal sphere." (Ling, 2008, p. 22)

When communicative behavior accomplishes a goal, communication is considered ***effective***. Each person, then, determines effectiveness because goals are often personal. This is not just about getting what we want; it is about communicating our messages clearly with an understanding of our audience. When we communicate effectively, we invite others to share in our point of view while we try to understand their perspectives. However, a principled person develops goals that are culturally and contextually appropriate and pays close attention to the well-being of those involved.

Communication Competence Grid

Morreale, Spitzberg, and Barge (2007) created a ***competence grid*** that explains how people enact varying degrees of appropriateness and effectiveness when communicating. For example, we might be appropriate, but not effective, which is called "***sufficing***" (p. 31), when we do not disturb a waiter to have our water glass refilled. We are kind but we do not quench our thirst; therefore our goal is not accomplished. On the other hand, we can be kind in our request for water, acting appropriately and effectively, which is called "***optimizing***" (Morreale et al., p. 31). Both of these behaviors involve following rules and the norms of the context—being appropriate—and they fall on the horizontal axis of Morreale et al.'s "competence grid" (p. 32). The vertical axis is devoted to the effectiveness of the interaction.

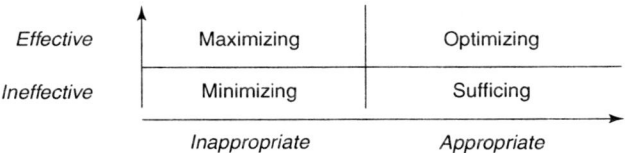

Figure 1.1 Competence grid.
Developed by Morreale et al. (2007) to help students visualize the relationship between appropriateness and effectiveness.

When your behavior is both inappropriate and ineffective, you are exhibiting "***minimizing***" (Morreale et al., 2007, p. 31) behavior. For example, if you want to pass an exam, but ignore a "no cell phone policy" in class by texting instead of taking notes, and subsequently fail your exam, you exhibit minimizing behavior. Your behavior would have been both inappropriate *and* ineffective because you did not follow class rules and did not reach your goal.

Shouting at a food service worker to get pizza, and receiving the pizza, is "***maximizing***" (Morreale et al., 2007, p. 31) behavior. It is effective because you receive the pizza but it is inappropriate because you belittled the worker. In both of these scenarios, the behavior is inappropriate, so would these behaviors be ethical? What is ethical behavior? If we define **ethics** as values in action, would these behaviors line up with your values?

Throughout this textbook, we ask you to reflect on how humans constitute ethical communication and what it means to live a principled life. Perhaps thinking about our communicative behavior as being both appropriate and effective will encourage us to ask difficult questions about our communicative behaviors. Each section below explores how the components of communication competence (*motivation, knowledge,* and *skills*) affect our interactions.

HOW DOES *MOTIVATION* BUILD COMMUNICATION COMPETENCE?

Thinking about how many problems can be addressed with communication skills can motivate us to communicate competently. Spitzberg (2011) proposed that motivation involves an "approach and avoidance orientation to communication" (p. 147); that is, it involves whether or not you enjoy and/or look forward to communicating with others. Some people may be eager to communicate with friends but they shy away from large social gatherings and public speaking; others look forward to the energy that they feel after presenting and meeting with new people.

> Manchester University (2013) includes the following values in its mission statement: "learning, faith, service, integrity, diversity, and community" (para. 2).
> What values would you include if asked to create a university values statement? If we get food from the food service worker, but we belittle the worker, are we acting in accordance with Manchester values? In light of Manchester's mission statement, would we be using our "education and faith to lead principled, productive, and compassionate lives that improve the human condition?" (para. 1)

Personality Style and Motivation to Communicate

Cain (2012) described how personality affects our motivations to communicate. She observed that *introverts* prefer to listen deeply to one message at a time, reflect before responding, and use language precisely. She clarified that they are not necessarily shy, but that they sometimes express themselves better in writing than in conversation and often look forward to solitude as "me time." She wrote that introverts "may have strong social skills and enjoy parties and business meetings, but after a while wish they were home in their pajamas" (p. 11). Introverts may avoid contexts where prompt, abrupt interactions are the norm, and where large groups of strangers might argue. In the classroom, introverts probably won't jump into debates or blurt out answers, but they might just have a list of questions to discuss with the professor afterward.

Cain noted that, in contrast to introverts, *extroverts* enjoy multiple, casual messages, like to "think out loud and on their feet," reply promptly, and "prefer talking to listening" (p. 11). She wrote how extroverts can be the life of the party and probably won't let your messages die in their inboxes. In the classroom, extroverts are often energized by banter, eager to participate, and a little worried about an extended, dull session with the professor during office hours.

Cain also described *ambiverts*, whose motivations to communicate are somewhere between those of introverts and extroverts. Cain stressed that sometimes ambiverts are introverts coping in an extrovert-dominated culture; they can be overstimulated, forced-to-multi-message introverts who, given their druthers, would prefer a quiet office or studio to today's door-less, shared workspaces. In the classroom, ambivert behavior may vary depending on the class and the structure.

Listening is Ethical

Communication researchers have suggested that—irrespective of personality—*listening* to another person is the ethical thing to do (e.g., Beard, 2009; Lipari, 2009; Shotter, 2009). Listening is "the process of receiving, constructing meaning from, and responding to spoken and/or nonverbal messages" (International Listening Association, 1996). We need to listen to others to create meaning. Shotter (2009) proposed that human beings need each other to find meaning, as a collective and as individuals:

> For, without a shared [sense] of determining surroundings, people, literally, do not know "where they are," they lack orientation, they do not know what to expect of those around them. In other words, if we and our interlocutors are to communicate readily and easily, we rely on those with whom we are involved to sustain between us the sense of a collective-we, a shared reality that is *our* jointly shared reality. And it is only in relation to such a jointly shared reality that we can express to each other *who* we are, express the nature of our unique inner lives to each other. Thus, we owe our very being, our identity, to it. If it collapses, if there is a lack of a jointly shared reality, then it is quite easy for us to feel unheard, or unable to express ourselves. (p. 40)

Rawlins (2003) advocated for a moral imperative when listening to others. He suggested that to listen to others, it is necessary to postpone our own speaking and to be genuinely open to hearing the other person. He described listening as a "committed, active passivity" (p. 123) that ultimately leads to personal change:

> Hearing comes first. Hearing comes before speaking. In this context, your hearing speaks louder than your saying. It announces and makes possible who you are and who you are trying to become. Dedicated listening enacts a suspended or altered context of power. It is a form of surrender, a vulnerability and susceptibility to others... (p. 123)

How do these researchers affect your thinking about finding the motivation to interact with others? What other personal motivation do you have? What would your friends add to this list?

WHAT *KNOWLEDGE* BUILDS COMMUNICATION COMPETENCE?

In addition to motivation, you need to understand what is involved when people communicate; you need knowledge about how to effectively communicate across contexts. We begin with what is involved when people communicate. Draw a picture of two people communicating. What did you include besides humans with mouths and ears? Crossed arms? Cell phones?

If you included mouths and ears on your stick figures, you indicated that humans are both ***senders (S)*** and ***receivers (R)*** of verbal ***messages (M)***. Did you include any nonverbal behaviors, such as arms crossed or hands extended? Nonverbal cues and words can both be considered ***channels (C)***, or media through which people send and receive messages. Channels can be mediated as well, which is why some people might have included cell phones, computers, and/or televisions in their drawings.

These elements are part of an early model of communication, called the ***information transfer model***. Engineer Claude Shannon first developed this model in 1948 as a part of information theory. Although the model was developed to describe human–machine

CYBER-FEEDBACK

Today's interactive media make use of feedback that is provided by users, or even by people or objects that are simply detectable. Websites alter their appearances, Netflix serves up ads, smart homes turn on the lights and adjust the temperature, and drones alter their flight plans in response to passively—or even unknowingly—provided feedback.

Such uses of feedback are consistent with the prefix "cyber" that is in words such as "cyberspace," "cyberpunk," "cybernetics," and "cyberculture." *Cyber* is rooted in the Greek adjective for "steering" or "governing" and gestures to the ways machines use feedback to direct and control spaces, messages, and even people.

Have you noticed that when you visit websites or make purchases with a credit card, that ads for those things appear on your phone, or even through postal mail? Have you noticed that when you log into the free Wi-Fi, an ad for a nearby business pops up on your phone? What forms of feedback do you provide without even thinking about doing so?

and machine–machine communication, the components adapt easily to human communication. It later became known as the Shannon–Weaver model (Weaver & Shannon, 1963).

In addition to the sender, receiver, and message, this adapted version of the Shannon–Weaver model also includes concepts of ***encoding*** (the meaning that the sender puts in the message), ***decoding*** (the meaning that the receiver grasps), ***noise*** (environmental sounds, physiological distractions, and semantic interference), and ***feedback*** (an indication from the receiver of how the sender's message was interpreted) to show communication as an interactive process (Figure 1.2).

Add these four new concepts to your drawing of two people communicating. Be sure to include marks that indicate the environmental, physiological, and semantic noises affecting the sender, receiver, channel, and the encoding and decoding processes. For example, the lightning bolt through channel and message could refer to "semantic" interference. If you do not know what "semantic" means, you are experiencing ***semantic noise***—interference caused by not knowing the meaning of a word; in this case, "semantic." Similarly, ***physiological noise*** is any distraction that involves the body, such as hunger, fatigue, and illness. You can indicate semantic or physiological noise by drawing a lightning bolt through both the sender and receiver. Finally, ***environmental noise***

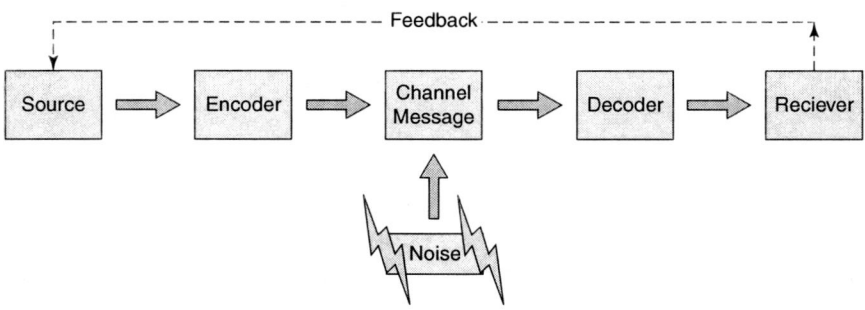

Figure 1.2 Shannon–Weaver information transfer model. This model presents communication as a linear process.

includes anything in the context that might affect speaking and listening: air conditioning or heating fans, people talking, keyboards clicking, and music playing.

Berlo (1960) expanded on Weaver and Shannon's (1963) model by including the same key elements of the transaction—SMCR—but he elaborated the complexity of each element (Figure 1.3). For Berlo, the ***source*** (sender) and ***receiver*** both interact with a unique set of communication skills, attitudes, knowledge, and position within a *cultural* system.

Think about entering a new job and communicating with your supervisor; your supervisor has a different level of knowledge and a higher status than you. This difference in status may affect the way you communicate, especially if you and your supervisor have cultural differences (e.g., age, ethnicity, and/or religion). If you communicate with someone you do not care for, your attitudes will affect your communication.

The ***message*** is the content or information shared. However, the message also has a structure beyond just the content. When you construct messages, you make decisions about the kind of words to use and how you want to arrange them. When you build a persuasive presentation, you spend time arranging and selecting your most important arguments and forms of support to help listeners best understand your ideas.

The ***channel*** is the final key element to communication in the SMCR model. For instance, how are conversations via text message and face-to-face different? Are there some channels that you prefer to use for some purposes and not for others? If you have ever argued with someone through text messaging, you know how frustrating that channel can be. In this course, we communicate through a face-to-face channel, but you also could take a class online, or watch a video of a lecture, and you would receive messages through a different channel. Both reading and listening are channels. Mediated communication, such as television, film, websites, radio, magazines, and newspapers, are channels too.

Information transfer models have been criticized for their linear form, for implying that communication is only back and forth, one way at a time. That linear form does not reflect the way humans actually communicate face-to-face. When we listen to speakers, we engage in nonverbal behaviors that potentially communicate something to others; and when we speak, we simultaneously receive and process messages. Have you ever had a conversation with a friend who was texting on their phone or looking at a computer screen? Their nonverbal messages communicated a lack of interest, even if they did

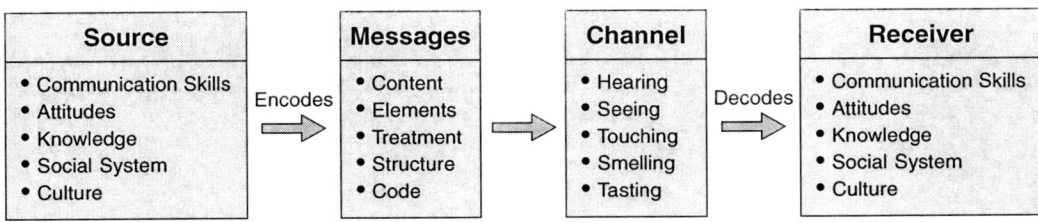

Figure 1.3 Berlo's SMCR model.
This model elaborates each element of the Shannon–Weaver model.

not intend to send that message. Positive nonverbal behaviors such as eye contact, nodding, and smiling can communicate interest in the ongoing conversation. Communicators adjust their approaches during the interaction; it is not only a linear back and forth. Communication is simultaneous, and we create messages even as we consume them.

Realizing the simultaneity of encoding and decoding for each person in an interaction, some communication scholars (e.g., Barnlund, 2008; Schramm, 1954; Watzlawick, Beavin, & Jackson, 1967) developed the ***transactional model*** of communication. The transactional model builds on the basic information transfer model by noting that we need to have a ***shared field of meaning***—some understanding of another's experiences, values, attitudes, and beliefs—to communicate. Because we all have different life experiences, values, attitudes, and beliefs, we cannot assume that others automatically share those same fields of meaning (although we often do make this assumption in communicating).

As we encode and decode messages, we apply our field of meaning to make sense of interactions. When we define communication as meaning creation, we develop a shared field of meaning. When your professor says she will return papers "soon," what does that mean to you? What do you think it means to your professor? Misunderstandings result from not sharing the same field of meaning about words, such as "soon" and "later." Communication can help you clarify and establish shared meanings.

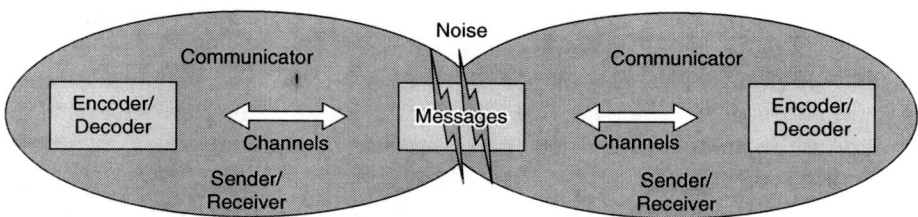

Figure 1.4 Transactional model.
This model demonstrates how we simultaneously encode and decode messages and share meaning.

The transactional model of communication suggests that messages are more than encoded information. We know that messages are both intentional and unintentional, and that they can be interpreted differently. Senders and receivers do not control the meanings of messages—meanings are created through interaction. Have you ever argued with someone who took a comment "the wrong way?" That would imply that the sender controls the meaning of the message. However, if you are the receiver, you know that the meaning you decode is also important. The transactional model of communication suggests we create meaning through interaction. A ***message***, then, is an action—intentional or not—to which we attach meaning. These actions can be verbal (written or spoken) or nonverbal. We may not always intend them. If you put your head down on your desk during a lecture because you are tired, the professor may attach the meaning that you are tired; however, the professor could also interpret your action as a message that you are bored or disrespectful. The transactional model reminds us that we always draw on our own fields of meaning, and we can create shared fields of meaning with competent communication.

Finally, models are lenses through which we can understand some facet of the world. Many models have been developed to explain communication, and each model has its explanatory powers and criticisms. There is not one "right" or true model. Some models apply readily to online communication, such as the Shannon–Weaver model, whereas other models make more sense for face-to-face interaction, such as the transactional model. The information transfer model downplays the importance of listening as an integral and ethical part of oral communication (Adams & Cox, 2010). The transactional model highlights how people simultaneously decode (listen) and encode (speak and gesture) messages throughout an interaction. However, neither model emphasizes the ethical imperative of trying to understand a message, just as vigorously as we try to be understood. Are you willing to work as hard to understand as you are to be understood? If so, then let us discover what skills we need.

WHAT *SKILLS* BUILD COMMUNICATION COMPETENCE?

Throughout this text, we will explore how effective and appropriate language and nonverbal behaviors build listening skills needed for each context. We begin with how to create an ***ethics*** (*values in action*) of listening. Beard (2009) proposed that people make a series of choices when communicating, and each choice involves ethical listening decisions. He believed that an investigation of these choices could serve as "a basis for evaluating the ethics of our communicative practice" (p. 7).

Listening Choices Involved in an Ethics of Listening

We adapted Beard's (2009) listening choices to demonstrate the choices we need to make in a classroom setting:

1. **The choice to listen (or NOT to listen):** Students recognize that a choice not to listen impacts immediate interactions and future opportunities to discuss these experiences. For example, when students choose to "tune out" a campus speaker discussing financial responsibility, they may miss relevant information. They may also lose the opportunity to discuss the speaker's ideas with others in the classroom and during dinner conversations.
2. **The choice to listen selectively (or NOT to listen selectively):** When students keep listening to a lecture for new information (not just tuning in for what they want to hear), they have the opportunity to encounter and discuss concepts and contexts that are unfamiliar to them. For example, students may not like to listen to National Public Radio (NPR), but when asked to do so by a professor or classmate, the student learns how current trends (e.g., the rising costs of emergency room visits) impact his/her life and the lives of classmates.

3. **The choice to listen together (or NOT to listen together):** When students pay attention to peers and professors in class, they feel part of something bigger than when they listen selectively and choose not to listen. Many times there are classroom stories and experiences that are integral to a student's development as a person of ability and conviction: listening creates community. For example, the class may discover that there are people who have fewer resources (e.g., financial, personal, and legal) and brainstorm ways the class can affect change. Similarly, students can learn from a classmate about physical limitations, challenging them to explore how they might be helpful to this classmate in the future (p. 18).

Beard (2009) proposed that when one has fully explored these choices, then one has developed an ethics of listening, acting both appropriately and effectively. With these deliberations, we know how to arrive at the choice to listen to another and to listen successfully. The decision to listen requires much effort and is dependent on context and purpose.

Listening Purposes and Contexts

We will find in each chapter different purposes for listening within each context. For example, in a public communication setting, we may listen to a symphony concert for the following purposes: *appreciative*—pleasure and enjoyment; *comprehensive*—understanding of a composition that we have studied in class; *critical*—analyzing the conductor's ability to change tempo; and/or *empathetic*—supporting a good friend who spent hours rehearsing (Worthington & Fitch-Hauser, 2012, pp. 23–34).

We hope these discussions about listening choices have renewed your motivation to gain more knowledge about ethical communication *skills* needed across contexts. As we discover the knowledge and skills needed to be competent communicators in *public* speaking situations (one-to-many), followed by *interpersonal* (one-on-one) interactions, and *small group* settings (three or more), we explore the impact of *language* and *nonverbal behaviors* on our ability to *listen* across cultures and contexts.

The ability to explain the ethical choices inherent in communication across contexts differentiates you from other university students. We believe that to lead principled lives, we do not just communicate with others; we also reflect on how we create meaning together. Ultimately, we hope that you lead productive and compassionate lives by implementing what you learn in the text and assessing the results of your communication efforts to determine whether you were both effective *and* appropriate in your communicative behaviors.

Conclusion

Human communication is human meaning making. To understand this definition is to recognize that previous assumptions we may have made about communication are inaccurate. A competent communicator knows what to say and do based on cultural rules and norms of a specific context. When we think about our communicative behavior as being both appropriate *and* effective, we ask difficult questions about what constitutes ethical communication: we look to optimize instead of maximize, minimize, or suffice.

In this chapter, we explored how motivation, knowledge, and skills build communication competence across cultures and contexts. We considered that motivation to communicate might depend on personality and the impetus to act in accordance with our values. We built knowledge about what occurs during the communication process, recognizing that we simultaneously send and receive messages. We moved beyond the information transfer models of human communication and found that a transactional model emphasizes how people simultaneously decode (listen) and encode messages to create meaning.

Ultimately, a transactional process of communication requires important listening skills, or an ethics of listening. We must make choices to listen and to listen to each other, choosing not to listen selectively, so that we can listen effectively based on purpose and context. With this foundational knowledge of the communication process, we are ready to explore how to be competent communicators in public communication contexts.

REFERENCES

Adams, W. C., and Cox, E. S. 2010. The teaching of listening as an integral part of an oral activity: an examination of public-speaking texts. *International Journal of Listening* 24:89–105. DOI:10.1080/10904011003744524

Barnlund, D. C. 2008. A transactional model of communication. In *Communication theory* (2nd ed.), ed. C. D. Mortensen, 47–57. New Brunswick, NJ: Transaction.

Beard, D. 2009. A broader understanding of the ethics of listening: philosophy, cultural studies, media studies and the ethical listening subject. *International Journal of Listening* 23:7–20. DOI:10.1080/10904010802591771

Berlo, D. K. 1960. *The process of communication: an introduction to theory and practice.* New York: Holt, Rinehart & Winston.

Cain, S. 2012. *Quiet: the power of introverts in a world that can't stop talking.* New York: Crown. International Listening Association. 1996. www.listen.org

Ling, R. 2008. *New tech, new ties: how mobile communication is reshaping social cohesion.* Cambridge, MA: The MIT Press.

Lipari, L. 2009. Listening otherwise: the voice of ethics. *International Journal of Listening* 23:44–59. DOI:10.1080/10904010802591888

Manchester University, North Manchester. 2013. *Mission statement.* Retrieved from www.manchester.edu/Common/AboutManchester/Mission.htm

McCroskey, J. C., Richmond, V. P., and McCroskey, L. L. 2006. *An introduction to communication in the classroom: the role of communication in teaching and training.* Boston, MA: Pearson.

Morreale, S. P., Spitzberg, B. H., and Barge, J. K. 2007. *Human communication: motivation, knowledge, & skills.* 2nd ed. Belmont, CA: Thomson Wadsworth.

Rawlins, W. K. 2003. Hearing voices/learning questions. In *Expressions of ethnography*, ed. R. P. Clair, 119–25. Albany: SUNY Press.

Schramm, W. 1954. How communication works. In *The process and effects of communication*, ed. W. Schramm, 3–26. Urbana: University of Illinois Press.

Shotter, J. 2009. Listening in a *way* that recognizes/realizes the world of "the other." *International Journal of Listening* 23:21–43. DOI:10.1080/10904010802591904

Spitzberg, B. H. 1983. Communication competence as knowledge, skills, and impression. *Communication Education* 32: 323–29. DOI:10.1080/03634528309378550

Spitzberg, B. H. 2011. The interactive media package for assessment of communication and critical thinking (IMPACCT©): testing a programmatic online communication competence assessment system. *Communication Education* 60, 145–73. DOI:10.1080/03634523.2010.51 8619

Spitzberg, B. H., and Cupach, W. R. 1984. *Interpersonal communication competence.* Beverly Hills, CA: Sage.

Trenholm, S., and Jensen, A. 2013. *Interpersonal communication.* 7th ed. New York: Oxford University Press.

Watzlawick, P., Beavin, J. H., and Jackson, D. D. 1967. *Pragmatics of human communication: a study of interactional patterns, pathologies, and paradoxes.* New York: Norton.

Weaver, W., and Shannon, C. E. 1963. *The mathematical theory of communication.* Urbana: University of Illinois Press.

Worthington, D. L., and Fitch-Hauser, M. E. 2012. *Listening: processes, functions, and competency.* New York, NY: Allyn & Bacon.

CHAPTER 2
PUBLIC COMMUNICATION

LEARNING OBJECTIVES

By the end of this chapter, you should be able to:

- Explain the purposes of a persuasive speech.
- Analyze your audience and speaking situation and describe why audience analysis is important.
- Explain how the five canons of rhetoric contribute to an effective speech and apply them in your own speech.
- Explain the differences between inductive and deductive reasoning.
- Identify the forms of reasoning and provide examples of each.
- Describe how logical fallacies hinder effective reasoning and provide original examples.
- Develop a speech plan.
- Describe effective and appropriate physical and vocal delivery.
- Give appropriate and effective speech criticism.

WHAT RESPONSIBILITIES DO COMMUNICATORS HAVE IN PUBLIC COMMUNICATION CONTEXTS?

Public communication involves one person speaking to many. Books about public speaking focus on presenters' actions, such as speech preparation, organization, and delivery. There are sections about analyzing and engaging audience members, and about adapting to the timing and location of the presentation. Are these topics familiar to you? How much instruction have you had in speech preparation? Do you have oral presentation skills?

Have you explored how oral communication skills differ from written communication skills? Perhaps you think the answer to this question is obvious; for instance, written messages contain "periods" and "paragraphs" to indicate completion of thoughts and introduction of new thoughts, whereas oral communication relies on verbal transitions, such as "first" and "next," to move listeners through a speech. Moreover, great presenters weave stories and develop ideas; they do not just read lengthy sentences with big words. However, how many speakers have you heard who read a manuscript in a public setting, acting as if there is no difference between written and oral style?

Adams and Cox (2010) argued that because oral communication is unique, the "critical factors defining the dynamic of a spoken presentation should impact all aspects of speech preparation" (p. 91). We agree and, consequently, in this chapter we place the burden on speakers and listeners alike. As a speaker, you can aid listeners by preparing a few main ideas and using a variety of supporting material, as "the variety not only helps listeners understand but helps speakers because they are not focusing on covering material but rather upon getting the audience to understand the idea" (Adams & Cox, 2010, p. 100). As a listener, you can influence the speaker by paying close attention, by making the choices that listeners make each time they "tune in" (Beard, 2009).

As we discuss persuasive speeches, we begin with the speaker's tasks and explore how to develop, support, organize, and deliver ethically appropriate and effective messages.

AS A SPEAKER, HOW DO I DISCOVER WHICH IDEAS TO PRESENT?

How do you create a speech that is focused on ideas? How do you create an effective and appropriate speech? We grapple with these important questions in light of persuasive speaking. We first define persuasive speeches and describe their purpose; then we show how the canons of rhetoric are a model for speech development.

Morreale, Spitzberg, and Barge (2007) defined **persuasive speech** as speaking with the intent to "influence an audience's attitudes, beliefs, values or behaviors and moving listeners to change or to action of some kind" (p. 278). Persuasive speeches have three purposes: (1) to reinforce the beliefs of an audience who already agrees with you, (2) to change the beliefs or attitudes of an audience, and/or (3) to move an audience to action. For example, persuasive speeches encourage behavioral changes, such as donating money to a charity or volunteering time with a community organization. They also encourage attitudinal changes, such as excitement for food plan choices and accessible campus parking lots.

Speakers should be cautious when they intend their speeches to change attitudes or beliefs. Such speeches require a comprehensive understanding of audiences and a careful use of appealing and values-supporting materials. Changing deeply held attitudes or beliefs through a speech is highly unlikely, regardless of a speaker's caution. For example, you could give a well-crafted speech with plenty of relevant and authoritative support that argues the New York Yankees are a better baseball team than are the Chicago Cubs, but if we are Cubs fans, there is no amount of statistical information or opinion that is going to make us Yankees fans.

Salient (relevant to you) beliefs are deeply ingrained in our values and attitudes. Political affiliations, religious convictions, and opinions on hot-button social issues, such as abortion and gun control, are part of your salient beliefs. Are you likely to change your opinion on one of these issues because of one speech given by a classmate? Probably not.

While we should avoid some topics for class speeches if they would involve attempts to change salient beliefs, it is important to establish *salience* for your audience. This means that the topic should relate to the audience members. When speaking briefly to a diverse audience (such as your peers in this class), prepare a speech that persuades the audience to take action or make a reasonable, small change; trying to change salient beliefs within such a context is often inappropriate and is rarely effective.

Audience and Situational Analysis

In order to persuade an audience, you have to know a little about who they are and their attitudes and beliefs. *Audience analysis* is about discovering as much as possible about your audience for the purpose of listening-centered communication. You should know something about their *personal characteristics*. For example, you might group audience members into similar age ranges. However, not everyone is from the same socio-economic class or is interested in the same topics. Try not to assume that all of your audience members are the same because their personal characteristics are the same. Imagine that you are preparing a speech on safe sex practices. You probably want to know if your audience is mostly college students or, say, seniors from a local retirement home, because you will approach your speech differently.

You might also want to get a sense of the audience's *attitudes* and *beliefs* toward your topic. For example, if you are considering giving a speech on smoking cessation, but no one in your audience smokes, it will not be a meaningful speech of action. To determine the values and attitudes of your audience, you might consider surveying your audience ahead of time or asking knowledgeable others for background on the group. If you are to speak to a group of faculty members about a university policy, it would be helpful to interview a few faculty members before developing your speech. Doing so will help you understand their attitudes toward that policy.

Finally, analyze the speaking *situation*. Think about the factors that are going to affect your speech, such as *time* and *place*. What are some of the factors here that you might need to plan for? What might you need to know about a speaking situation beyond who the audience might be? Consider the time of day, the setup of the room, the technology you might need to use, lighting, and ambient noise. Giving a speech in a classroom and

> **AUDIENCE AND SITUATIONAL ANALYSIS INCLUDES**
> - Personal characteristics
> - Attitudes and beliefs
> - Time and place

giving a speech in the middle of the campus mall with a bullhorn are very different experiences. Thinking through these issues ahead of time can reduce anxiety about the speaking situation.

Rhetoric and the Rhetorical Canons

Communication scholars trace effective persuasive speaking to ancient Greek philosophers in the fourth and fifth centuries B.C.E., when oratory was a key part of Greek political life. Seasoned orators trained men from a young age to influence others through speech. Such training was crucial for success in Greek democracy and civil affairs. The Greeks established this persuasive practice, which was known as **rhetoric**: the ability to understand the situation and use the available and appropriate means of persuasion (Aristotle, 1909/1990).

The Greek oral tradition still impacts the way we prepare persuasive messages. In order to persuade, we must be attentive to what resonates with each unique audiences. We must use what is available to us as speakers, which includes our credibility and ethics (***ethos***), emotional appeals to the audience (***pathos***), and sound reasoning and evidence (***logos***). Aristotle's **rhetorical canons**—five essential activities needed for persuasive speech preparation and presentation—frame the discussion below. We begin with discussions of *invention* and *arrangement* (organization), and then discuss *style, memory,* and *delivery*.

> **ARISTOTLE'S NICOMACHEAN ETHICS**
>
> Aristotle believed persuasion was a neutral tool that could serve both noble and nefarious ends. However, he also maintained that those who would persuade, "should be able to argue persuasively on either side of a question, not that we may actually do both (for one should not persuade what is debased) but in order that it may not escape our notice what the real state of the case is and that we ourselves may be able to refute it if another person uses speech unjustly" (as cited in Carman, 2006, p.17).
>
> Aristotle took this a step further when he suggested that ethics were not merely mental exercises, but that they were a way of life. He referred to this way of life as *Nicomachean Ethics*. At Manchester University, becoming a person of ability of conviction means living ethically, and being as eager to be persuaded as to persuade.
>
> When you seek to persuade, do you have the ability to give other points of view a fair and accurate hearing? Do you have the conviction to live according to the principles and values you advocate to others?

AS A SPEAKER, HOW DO I USE *INVENTION*?

The first step in speech preparation is to "invent" a speech topic, which requires you to add your unique perspective to a general, persuasive topic, and to develop your topic for an audience. For example, if you spend many hours in a canine club as a member of 4H, your firsthand experience will influence the way you approach a persuasive speech about dog shelters. What experiences have you had that provide a unique approach to a topic? Have you had athletic or musical experiences? Have you had health challenges? Have you overcome difficulties in your family?

Think about what you know, but also about what will interest the audience. Consider the constraints of the occasion. Can you handle this topic within a limited time frame? Even if a topic is given to you, decide how you will approach it in a unique way.

For example, you have five minutes to give a persuasive speech to an audience of high school students in Cordier auditorium on the topic of, "Why they should attend Manchester University." Even though you have a general topic and a purpose to move the audience to action, you still need to narrow and develop the topic. What will you talk about that will persuade your audience?

Reasoning

Once you select a topic, consider how you will persuade your audience. Understanding logic and the forms of reasoning will help you develop a sound argument. These concepts are useful not only for your speech but also for your writing and everyday communication. See if you can identify these forms of logic the next time you read an editorial or hear a persuasive argument.

When constructing an argument, think of this formula: *Argument = Assertion + Support*. The assertion is the main claim you want to make. The support can come in various forms. Some of your support will be in the form of evidence, using data and testimony. We will explore that in the next section. Support also comes in the form of sound reasoning. This is where you establish logos. Let us begin by differentiating between inductive and deductive logic.

Deductive vs. Inductive Logic

In ***deductive logic***, a person makes a claim or assertion based on some premise that is generally accepted by the audience. This is called "top down" logic. Deduction follows a logic structure called a ***syllogism*** that has three parts: a major premise, a minor premise, and a conclusion. The major premise is a generally accepted statement. The minor premise is a specific instance. If all of the premises are true, then it follows that the conclusion must be true and the syllogism is valid. Here is an example (Cavender & Kahane, 2013, p. 10):

> Everything made of copper conducts electricity. (Major premise)
> This wire is made of copper. (Minor premise)
> Therefore this wire will conduct electricity. (Conclusion)

The above syllogism is valid because both of the premises are true. It is possible for a syllogism to be logically sound but incorrect. For example,

> All dogs bark. (Major premise)
> Berkeley is a dog. (Minor premise)
> Therefore Berkeley barks. (Conclusion)

Logically, this argument seems to work. However, there are dogs that do not bark, so the major premise is incorrect. The syllogism can be used to map many arguments. In research, deductive logic is often used to confirm a narrow hypothesis. It is unusual to see a full syllogism as an argument in daily communication. Instead, one of the premises is usually missing, and the audience fills in the gap. This informal structure is called an **enthymeme**. For example, "this copper wire will conduct electricity" is missing the major premise.

Inductive logic is a "bottom up" approach; the presenter draws a conclusion based on a series of specific examples or instances. The conclusion in an inductive argument is never guaranteed—it is based on assumptions. For example, if you see three different squirrels that all try to attack you, you might come to the conclusion that all squirrels are mean.

Let us put this in the context of an argument in a persuasive speech on tuition hikes. You could tell the stories of three students who have faced difficulties staying in school because of tuition hikes. These would be your specific examples. You might then conclude that many students struggle to pay for college. This would be an assumption (not all students are concerned about tuition), but the conclusion is likely to be accepted by your audience as generally true. Listeners respond to messages on a satisfaction or need-based basis, not always on a rational basis.

Remember that starting with the general conclusion and applying to the specific case is deductive; starting with the specific case and moving to a general conclusion is inductive. Now that you understand the broad difference between inductive and deductive reasoning, we'll explore some specific patterns of reasoning.

Forms of Reasoning

Forms of reasoning are ways of arranging information to lead to a conclusion. Sometimes, your entire persuasive speech may be based on one of these forms; other times, the form of reasoning may be through an example that supports your overall point. While there are many types of reasoning, the following types are common in oral persuasion.

Argument by Definition: An argument by definition posits that something meets previously agreed upon criteria. This argument can be simple if the criteria are based on facts, but is more complex if based on values. We can agree on the defining characteristics of a chair (legs, a surface for sitting), but do we agree on the defining characteristics of a good friend? Remember that meaning is co-created through communication. As we will explore when we discuss the canon of style, words do not always have a single correct meaning. The test of an argument by definition asks, "to what extent do we agree on the defining characteristics?"

For example, in the "pro-life"/"pro-choice" abortion debate, both sides make arguments based on the definition of "life." The debate exists, and cannot be resolved, because both sides cannot agree on the defining characteristics or criteria for what "life" is and when it begins. While both sides make arguments by definition, if they do not fundamentally agree on the criteria of that definition, the rest of the arguments are not persuasive.

Argument by Sign: A sign argument is based on the assumption that every thing, condition, or idea has characteristics that tell you whether or not it is present. For example, smoke is a sign of fire. The sign is a visible indicator of an unobservable conclusion. If one variable is used as proof of another variable, it is an argument by sign. Weather forecasts are examples of argument by sign (dark clouds are indicators of rain). Arguments by sign are similar to cause-effect arguments. However, signs do not cause things to happen—they indicate the presence of something. For example, although SAT scores are interpreted as a sign that a person is smart and will succeed in college, they do not cause a person's success. Such an argument, of course, can be contested on the grounds that college use SAT scores in the admissions process. However, the test of an argument by sign is, "to what extent is the sign an assurance of the conclusion?"

Argument by Cause: An argument by cause is also known as a cause-effect argument. Causal arguments propose a direct relationship between two things or events—the cause, or agent, is necessary to produce the effect. For example, a lack of studying for the exam is a direct cause of failing the exam. However, there may be multiple causes involved in an effect. For example, "the unemployment rate is so high (*effect*) because of tax hikes on businesses" (*cause*). There may be other reasons that the unemployment rate is high beyond taxes on businesses. Arguments by cause can be fallacious because they minimize complexities. When you hear arguments by cause, ask yourself, "is this cause necessary and sufficient for this effect?" and "are there alternate causes?" Usually there are. For example, you may hear arguments that playing violent video games (*cause*) leads to violent behaviors in children (*effect*). The test of an argument by cause asks, "Is there a direct relationship between the cause and effect? Is anything else required?"

Argument by Generalization: Generalization is also called rhetorical induction because it relies on inductive logic. In an argument by generalization, you assert that what is true of a sample is true of a population. For example, if you meet three members of the basketball team and they are all tall, you might generalize that all basketball players are tall. These generalizations can be drawn from a sample or from individual cases. Surveys, opinion polls, and focus groups are all ways to draw samples and are used to make claims about a broader population. Ideally, these samples should be qualitatively and quantitatively representative of the population, although this can be tricky to accomplish. If you poll a group of Manchester students for their opinions on housing options but only ask your floor of first-year students, you cannot make inferences from these data about the opinion of all Manchester students because you do not have a representative sample. Arguments by generalization should always be qualified by asking, "is the sample qualitatively and quantitatively representative of the population?".

Argument by Analogy: The basic premise of an argument by analogy is that as X is like Y in some regard, X will be like Y in another regard. The argument compares two situations and reasons that what is true in one case will also be true in another. Whether an argument by analogy is persuasive or not depends on the relevance of the points of similarity. Analogies can be literal or figurative. Literal analogies are factual comparisons between situations. For example, "If marijuana legalization worked in Colorado, it can work in Indiana too" is a literal analogy comparing Colorado to Indiana. Both share the similarities of being states, but what other points of similarity or difference might be important? Figurative analogies are imaginative comparisons of situations. North Carolina governor Jim Hunt (School Vouchers Undermine Education, 1999) made a figurative analogy when he argued, "School vouchers are like leeches. They drain the lifeblood—public support—from our schools" (p. 6A). When testing argument by analogy, ask "are all of the important points are compared" and "are all the compared points are important?

Logical Fallacies

Logical fallacies are essentially errors in logic that lead to false conclusions. They can be deliberate attempts to mislead, or they can be accidental. It is important to be able to identify them in the persuasive tactics of others as well as in your own arguments. Fallacious arguments might sound good, but you want to avoid logical fallacies because they undermine your arguments. There are many kinds of fallacies, but we will only explore a few common types. Be aware that sometimes an argument can contain more than one fallacy.

Cause-effect: fallacies are based on the argument-by-cause form of reasoning. These fallacies follow a logical form of reasoning, but their reasoning is incorrect or unverifiable.

- **Post hoc** (an abbreviation of "post hoc ergo propter hoc", or "after this, therefore, because of this") is a logical fallacy that presupposes that because one event happened, another event happened. This is how a lot of superstitions start. For example, "because it's Friday the 13th, I'm having a terrible day." Or "I did well on my test because I wore my lucky t-shirt." This is also known as the "false cause" fallacy because the cause-effect relationship has not been demonstrated.
- **Slippery slope** fallacies suggest that one event automatically leads to a series of other undesirable events. The event supposedly acts as a catalyst for a rapid descent, as down a slippery slope. This is also called the fallacy of dire consequences. For example, "if the city passes a law to ban smoking in bars and restaurants, soon they will pass a law taking away our ability to smoke outside, and then they will ban cigarettes altogether!" Using a slippery slope fallacy diverts attention away from the issue at hand and is not supported by evidence that such consequences would occur.

Whereas post hoc and slippery slope fallacies might seem similar, remember that post hoc deals with events that have already happened, and slippery slope deals with future events that might happen.

Generalization: fallacies are based in the argument-by-generalization form of reasoning.

- **Sweeping generalizations** cluster ideas, people, or objects into one group and imply that all the items in the group are the same. The fallacy here is that the argument is generalizing too broadly. For example, you might hear the argument, "elderly drivers are dangerous and should have their licenses taken away." This clusters all elderly drivers into a category of "dangerous." You can see how prejudices and stereotypes can be sweeping generalizations.

- **Hasty Generalizations** are similar to sweeping generalizations, but instead of generalizing too broadly, they are based on too little evidence to make the claim. For example, "my roommate said her philosophy class was hard, and the one I'm in is hard, too. All philosophy classes must be hard!" It is a fallacy to generalize about all philosophy classes based on the experiences of two people. Another example: "I have never experienced violence on campus, and neither has anyone I know, so it is a safe campus." This is an argument by generalization because it infers that individual cases (in this case, personal experiences) apply to a broader group. The fallacy here is that your experience may not be representative of all students' experiences.

Fallacies of irrelevance: attempt to divert or deflect an argument by including irrelevant information rather than responding to the main ideas.

- **Ad hominem** (to the person) fallacies attack the character or actions of a person instead of his or her arguments. For example, "don't listen to Mike, he dropped out of college." Or, "You support government-sponsored health care? You must be a socialist." These critiques can be extremely effective at diverting an argument. When conservative radio host Rush Limbaugh called Sandra Fluke a "prostitute" because she supported insurance companies covering contraceptive costs (Fard, 2012), he made an ad hominem attack. There are times when critique of a person's character or actions is legitimate, but only if their character or actions are directly related to the issue at hand.
- **Argumentum ad populum** (appeal to the people), also known as the bandwagon technique, relies on peer pressure. This fallacy makes an argument based on the popularity of something, and without giving evidence as to why. This fallacy is common in advertisements: "Soda brand X is preferred by more people than any other soda" (with the implication that if it is preferred by a majority, it must be good). Another example is, "Yoga is becoming more popular, so everyone should try it."

Now that we have explored forms of reasoning and logical fallacies, it is time to find appropriate material to support your argument.

Supporting Material

How do you normally conduct research? Do you just go to Google and type in some terms? Do you only search Wikipedia? These may not be your best sources for reliable and credible information. You need to use sources that your audience finds credible, as doing so helps establish your *ethos*, or your personal credibility as a speaker.

When you craft a speech to move the audience to action, you might not find sources that directly state your argument. Look, instead, for different ways to support your ideas. Depending on your topic, support might take various forms. You might use academic journal articles, newspaper or magazine articles (online or in print), interviews with credible individuals, websites of relevant organizations, and government websites. These sources should lend support to your main ideas.

In the example of the speech about why high school students should attend Manchester, what outside sources would you use? Journal articles may not be particularly useful, but interviews with administration and admissions staff, the Manchester website, and materials created by the University's Public Relations and Admissions departments may be excellent sources of supportive information.

For most topics, library databases that allow you to access peer-reviewed academic journals are the best sources of information. The challenge with many academic articles, however, is that you first have to figure out what the researchers actually mean. If you are not sure what an article means, consult a professor or a librarian who can help you find relevant sources that both you and your audience will understand.

Before you consider using any source, especially web sources, you must evaluate their credibility. Audiences are likely to perceive a peer-reviewed journal article or a large newspaper as credible and reliable, and the information is likely to be fact-checked. The same cannot be said for the information on many web pages. If you must seek sources on the web, the CRAAP (Currency, Relevance, Authority, Accuracy, Purpose) test provides some guidelines for evaluation (CSU-Chico, 2010):

- **Currency:** *How timely is this information?* Check websites for a publication date or a revision date. If your topic is in flux, or if relevant facts are changing frequently, check for the source date. For instance, what was reliable information about AIDS 20 years ago differs from what we know about AIDS today. You may use old information to provide context, but you need to make that use clear in your speech.
- **Relevance:** *How important is this information to my topic?* Consider the intended audience for this source, and the level of the information. It might be too simple or too complex for your needs.
- **Authority:** *Who is the source?* Who is the author? Is the author qualified? How do you know? The Centers for Disease Control's website, for example, would pass the authority test; a random blog that you find about home remedies for the flu would not.
- **Accuracy:** *How reliable is this information?* Consider the types of evidence that are used to support the argument. If a website has spelling and grammatical errors, consider that the information also might have errors. If possible, verify any information you find. Authority does not always mean accuracy; even large, well-respected news sources do not always get the information right (although they usually correct it quickly).
- **Purpose:** *Why does this information exist?* Consider whether the purpose of the website is to inform, persuade, or entertain. Is the article based on fact or opinion? Is it someone's bias? Some nonprofit organizations and websites have a clear bias, and you should be cautious about citing them. This does not mean that they do not provide

accurate or useful information, but whenever possible, track down the original source of the information. An original source may provide more balanced information than would an entertaining, persuasive secondary source. For example, PETA (People for the Ethical Treatment of Animals) may not be the best site for a persuasive speech on animals. Although the organization offers a lot of information, it also has a strong bias, and using biased sources can hurt your credibility with the audience.

A note about Wikipedia: it is common for students to begin the process of invention through Wikipedia. That is acceptable for topic exploration, but you should avoid relying on or citing Wikipedia as a primary source. This advice holds true for any website that allows anyone to submit content to it. Although these sources can be great starting points for developing a topic, anyone is free to edit the content at any time. Although it is likely that someone will eventually fix wrong information that is presented, it is impossible to say when it will be fixed. At any point, the validity of the information may be compromised. An author of this book had a student change the Wikipedia entry for his hometown by listing himself as the mayor, and it remained that way for over a year before it was corrected!

Many Wikipedia entries are well-written and contain citations that are available through the library, which is perfectly acceptable. Whenever possible, trace a citation back to its original source. If you are unsure how to find a cited source, consult a librarian. He or she can help you track down the information you need. Attention to detail avoids plagiarism and enhances your credibility.

AS A SPEAKER, HOW DO I USE *ARRANGEMENT* (ORGANIZATION)?

With credible resources in hand, speakers turn their attention to arranging this supporting material. Adams and Cox (2010) suggested that presenters "refine supporting material with the listeners' capabilities foremost in mind" (p. 92). This advice means first recognizing that listeners may not be able to focus on more than three main points. We apply this advice to our example about persuading prospective students to come to Manchester.

Begin by finding two or three common themes in your research. What ideas emerge from your experiences and research? We often tell prospective students that they will build both academic and personal connections that last a lifetime. Based on your decision to come to Manchester, what would be another important idea to share with prospective students?

Once you discover a few important ideas that you want to develop, explain these ideas to a classmate. How did he or she respond? In this process of talking with another person, you will discover how developing ideas for a presentation is similar to your "natural interaction patterns" (Adams & Cox, 2010, p. 101). More important, when you focus on helping listeners understand, you do not worry about remembering details; instead, you emphasize a few memorable stories, statistics, and research studies. Finding a number of ways to develop an idea helps listeners pay attention and remember. Speakers need to be somewhat redundant; they should use **repetition** because there are no paragraphs that listeners can refer back to, as readers can do in an essay.

Consequently, you need a variety of supporting materials to explain each main idea, in addition to explicit transitional phrases to move between different types of supporting material. This structure ensures that you "reinforce the richness of each idea and help the audience appreciate its significance" (Adams & Cox, 2010, p. 92). For example, how could you find support material for your speech to persuade prospective students to come to Manchester?

You could develop your first idea with two types of supporting material: (1) a personal testimony (e.g., from a current student) and (2) an interview with an expert (e.g., a professor). Tie these supporting materials together with transitional phrases such as "the *second* way to understand this idea" and "*now* that we are aware of this startling statistic, we will look at how a current professor confirms this statistic." Explicit ***transitions***, such ***as*** "next," "second," and "final," connect main ideas and supporting material within each main idea.

Speech Plan

As speakers develop persuasive presentations, they create plans. These plans include the types of introduction, supporting material, and conclusion speakers anticipate will resonate with listeners. The plan also includes key words to represent the essence of the supporting material used to develop each main idea (e.g., interview, statistic, and/or testimony for each main idea). These key words represent the essence of the testimony (or interview or statistic), and indicate how such material will be salient for listeners. To demonstrate how this works, we will complete a speech plan for a presentation to prospective students.

First, we explore what type of ***introduction*** is needed for our audience: what will catch prospective students' attention? Attention getting devices can take the form of rhetorical questions (questions asked to get the audience thinking, not for direct answers), startling statistics (from research articles), personal stories (from interviews), digital media (YouTube videos), pictures (from marketing brochures), and quotations (from famous people). Which of these devices catch your attention? What others can you add?

For our presentation to prospective students, we decide to begin with a picture of students studying together in the Sisters Café from the Manchester University website. We propose that we can catch attention and create salience by suggesting that these friends met at student orientation during their first year at Manchester. This moves the prospective student from thinking about what campus life might be to seeing what happens at Manchester.

The final part of an introduction is the *preview*—a roadmap for where listeners are headed in the speech. A concise statement of main ideas allows the listener to know that he or she needs to understand just two or three things about life at Manchester. This

> I. Introduction
>   A. Picture of current students from Manchester website
>   B. Describe how students met their first year at Manchester
>   C. Preview of main ideas: Academic Connections and Personal Connections
>
> II. Main Ideas and Supporting Materials
>   A. *First,* Academic Connections
>   1. Professor interview
>   2. *In addition,* Startling statistic from research article
>   3. *Finally,* Personal experience with study abroad
>
>   *Now that you see the academic connections, let us explore the personal connections.*
>
>   B. *Second,* Personal Connections
>   1. Current student story
>   2. *In addition,* Pictures from Manchester website
>   3. *Finally,* Newspaper article about networking
>
> III. Conclusion
>   A. Summary of main ideas: Academic Connections and Personal Connections
>   B. Picture of current students from Manchester website

Figure 2.1 Speech plan.
This sample plan identifies essential elements such as the Introduction, Main Ideas and Supporting Materials, and the Conclusion, in addition to transitional phrases and words.

is especially helpful when listeners have difficulty paying attention due to the physical, environmental, and semantic noise described in Chapter 1.

A clear preview, along with numerous transitions, allows a listener who has drifted away to reenter the main ideas at any time. As a speaker, it is a relief to know that a preview and a transition can also help you remember how supporting material connects to the main ideas. We advise you to write transitional phrases into your speech plans, so that you will not forget to include them during a presentation (see words and sentences in italics in Figure 2.1).

The final piece of the speech plan is the **conclusion**. The conclusion and the introduction include the same pieces of information, but in reverse order. After reiterating the main points, you can return to your attention getting device, or use another one, such as quotation, for closure.

AS A SPEAKER, HOW DO I USE *STYLE* (LANGUAGE)?

What types of stories resonate with listeners? What words do they understand? What vivid images enhance their understanding? Style is the canon that focuses on how presenters use language to create meaning. In this section, we explore how to use concrete and figurative language that is both appropriate and effective.

As we discovered in Chapter 1, words help us create meaning with others. Unfortunately, we may not always agree on the meaning of the words. This disagreement occurs because meaning is not in the word, per se, but is instead in our experiences. For instance, if you and a friend each think about the word "dog," then disclose what type of dog you each imagined, you soon discover you did not have the same "***referent***" (e.g., your referent was a Golden Retriever and your friend's referent was a Dalmatian) for the "***symbol***" (the word "dog") because the "***reference***" (your thoughts, your friend's thoughts) is different.

Similarly, the two of you may feel differently about a "dog." If you snuggle with your Golden each evening before going to bed, then you think of dogs as companions (Figure 2.2). However, if a Dalmatian bit your friend while she was riding her bicycle, then she might think about the injury and her fear of dogs. Ogden and Richards (1946) proposed that meaning resides in people, and not in words, because each person imagines a different kind of dog based on their lived experiences. Ogden and Richards created a "triangle of reference" (p. 11), often referred to as a "triangle of meaning," to remind people that meaning is in the person. They argued that there is an indirect relationship (which is indicated by a dotted line) between the symbol and the referent.

Concrete Language

How does the triangle of meaning affect what language, and, consequently, what style we choose for listeners? Knowing that distinct, but related, meaning resides in

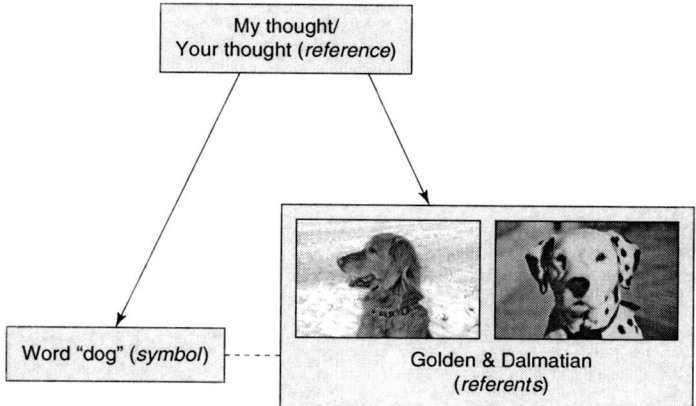

Figure 2.2 Triangle of reference (triangle of meaning).
This diagram was adapted from Ogden and Richards's "Referent of Meaning," which demonstrate how meaning resides in the person and not in the word. The dotted line between the symbol and the referents indicates that there is no meaning without reference, (our thoughts).

each person, we need to use language that ties directly to our listeners' experiences—concrete examples and vocabulary that resonate with listeners. For example, when you tell someone "I love you," how do they know what you mean? How do you know what they mean if they say it back? Have you ever heard the phrase "I love you but I'm not in love with you?" How can the word "love" encompass so many things? The word "love" does not have a concrete referent, and our references/thoughts about love may not match.

Haney (1992) refers to this phenomenon as bypassing. Haney writes that bypassing occurs when as ***bypassing***: "the listener presumably heard the same words that the speaker said, but the communicators seem to have talked past each other" (p. 268). The listener and speaker act as if the words mean the same thing to each person, but their interpretations are different. Similarly, communicators can use different words to refer to the same thing: some call a soft drink "soda," whereas others refer to it as "pop." Miscommunication often results because these assumptions are faulty and go unnoticed.

Furthermore, words may have multiple meanings. The word "nut," for example, is a word that depends on context—the word is not the thing it represents, and the connection between the word and the referent is arbitrary. Using concrete language can create a vivid picture for listeners, so it is important to remember that language choices reflect our assumptions and experiences, not necessarily those of our audience.

Sometimes abstract language can be used to strong persuasive effect. Listen to a political speech and pay attention to the abstract terms used: "freedom, liberty, justice, security," and so forth. These terms do not have concrete referents, but culturally we make positive mental associations with them. Burke (1969) called such terms "God-terms" because they are held in such high regard and represent ideals. There are also "devil-terms" that represent ultimate repulsion, such as "terrorism or un-American." While these terms can be persuasive, consider whether it is ethical to use these terms and if your audience holds the same understanding of the term that you do.

Figurative Language

We can draw listeners in with figurative language. We have already learned about analogy as a form of reasoning; let us see how simile, metaphor, and alliteration can contribute to listeners' comprehension of your ideas.

Listeners appreciate these figures of speech because they learn by comparison. For example, a ***simile*** uses the words "like" or "as" to compare items that are not alike. In our persuasive speech example, we might use a simile by suggesting that finding an academic major is like finding your favorite frozen yogurt by using one small tasting spoon at a time. A ***metaphor***, then, is a simile without the use of those two words: academic major exploration is a hike through a beautiful forest.

How might you use these two figures of speech to help us understand your ideas? Remember that an ***analogy*** is a comparison between two things based on similarities or resemblances between them.

AS A SPEAKER, HOW DO I USE *DELIVERY* (NONVERBAL CUES) AND *MEMORY*?

How can appropriate attire and gestures enhance your credibility? Have you seen speakers keep eye contact with listeners and use vocal variety to connect with listeners? We address these issues and more as we explore the *delivery* canon—physical delivery (e.g., appearance, posture, eye contact, and presentational aids) and vocal delivery (e.g., rate and inflection)—in addition to a discussion of the *memory* canon. We end this section with a discussion about speech criticism: how to make the most of peer feedback about your persuasive presentation.

Physical Delivery

Some of us may not like to admit that appearance is an important part of delivery. Because we learned at an early age that "clothes do not make the person," we avoid assigning importance to clothing. And yet how many of us know that professional attire contributes to a speaker's credibility? Similarly, in the United States, we encourage applicants for a new job to be well-prepared for questions *and* to be well-groomed. This means that the candidate is wearing clean clothing that is wrinkle-free and appropriate for the setting. Clothing and other objects that communicate messages about you are a part of nonverbal communication called **artifacts**. Think about how the t-shirt you are wearing, the cell phone you are carrying, or the accessories you have might send messages to others. While a business suit and briefcase might convey a serious, professional attitude, torn jeans, a baseball cap, and a backpack might convey a casual attitude.

For classroom speaking, we encourage students to be comfortable, but to avoid clothing with distracting words, logos, or styles. We also challenge them to explore what professional attire might contribute to their overall delivery. For instance, we find that when students modify their appearance, they may feel more like professionals, standing taller and taking a professional stance. We have also found that people are less likely to lean on the podium when wearing formal attire than when wearing a sweat suit and tennis shoes.

In addition to good posture, speakers should consider **kinesics**, or nonverbal cues that involve the body. *Gestures* and *body movements* should be meaningful and should highlight important points in the speech. For example, you might move toward listeners when you ask a question and make a key point. You also might use your hands to indicate numbers and size, so that listeners will have important reference points.

Equally as important as appropriate gestures and body movement are appropriate *facial expressions* and *eye contact*. Smiling and keeping direct eye contact with listeners are important norms in the United States. When we look listeners in the eye and extend a genuine smile, we communicate "honesty, openness, and respect for others—all crucial aspects of credibility" (Morreale et al., 2007, p. 329). We find that if we do not connect with listeners, then we give the opportunity to focus on other issues.

Finally, because listeners do not have manuscripts of our presentation, we need to help them follow the idea development in the presentation. As we learned with "arrangement" (e.g., transitions and repetition) and "style" (e.g., concrete and figurative language), redundancy helps listeners grasp the new ideas we are teaching them. We can use **presentational aids** such as PowerPoint or Prezi, handouts or handwriting on the board, and music or YouTube videos to provide an audio and/or visual "map" of the presentation. Much like new paragraphs in a written essay help readers, presentational aids serve as pointers for listeners in public communication.

Vocal Delivery

In addition to physical delivery, speakers pay close attention to vocal delivery—an area of nonverbal communication called **vocalics**. As listeners, we appreciate an enthusiastic *tone* of voice and a clear *articulation* of words. Even if we know better than to be monotone, sometimes we feel like impostors when we add the emphasis needed for public presentations. However, we need to use our "stage voices" (not our "inside voices" as our elementary teachers used to reprimand) to provide the enthusiasm and clear pronunciation that will reach the back of the classroom or meeting room.

Similarly, this stage voice includes speaking loud enough for everyone in the room to hear us. Some of us feel like we are shouting to reach the *volume* needed to make it beyond the first two rows of our audience. Lunceford (2007) argued that scientists and rhetorical theorists need to work together to demonstrate how all of these *aural* qualities work together for persuasion:

> The aural qualities of speech are powerful elements of persuasion. By incorporating elements of the poetic—repetition, formulaic construction, and vocal range and quality—a speaker can entrance the listener and increase the potential for persuasion both through the construction of ethos and through the skillful inducement of emotion. (p. 99)

As Lunceford explained, developing these aural qualities can enhance your ethos and pathos and can encourage the audience to pay attention to your message. Furthermore, we need to properly use **grammar** and **gender-neutral** language. As we discuss in the next section, we can have peers listen to our speeches as we practice so that grammatical errors and condescending language are noted, and consequently removed.

PRESENTATION AIDS AND PERSUASION

When you consider presentational aids, think of how they can help you use ethos, pathos, and logos. Will images and sounds help audience members remember and feel your message? Will touching an object help listeners connect with your ideas? Will charts, graphs, and handouts enhance your credibility or help people understand the weight of your evidence? What about the news clipping from your audience's hometown newspaper?

You should not use presentational aids for their sheer value as spectacle, or under the assumption that, "that which appears is good, that which is good appears" (Debord, 1983, p. 9). If a presentational aid does not contribute to your credibility, engage your audience emotionally, or enhance your use of reasons and evidence, it probably doesn't belong in your speech. In fact, it might just be a source of environmental noise.

Memory

When Aristotle spoke of "memory" as a canon of rhetoric, he did not just mean mnemonic devices to help you memorize a speech (although memorized speeches were quite common in ancient Greece—and they were even hours long!). Memory is linked to invention—to things you know and want to communicate. Memory is not just about knowing your speech it is also about knowing your message, which allows you to speak extemporaneously.

In an ***extemporaneous speech***, you are prepared and know your argument and supporting information, but you do not read from a ***manuscript*** and do not ***memorize*** your speech. There is nothing wrong with a manuscript speech if it is appropriate for the situation, when exact wording is important, and it is delivered well. However, learning to speak from limited notes is an important skill in college and in the workplace. If you are well-versed in your topic, your speech will be less rigid because you can adapt to your audience.

Many students are nervous about delivering extemporaneous speeches. They worry they will forget their speech or freeze up in front of the audience. Some students mistakenly believe that "winging it" with no preparation would be more effective than practicing. Speeches without adequate practice often seem disorganized and choppy to the listener. The best way to reduce ***speech anxiety*** is first to choose a *topic* you care about. If it is a message you want to deliver to the audience, your knowledge and enthusiasm for the topic will be reflected in your delivery. It is also essential to *practice* often. When possible, practice in the space where you will deliver the speech. Practice for a small audience such as roommates or friends. The more you practice, the more comfortable you will be with your content and the smoother your delivery will be.

What kind of delivery and style would you use to present to high school students about Manchester? Would you make it conversational or more formal? Would you use note cards or work from memory? These important choices about *delivery* and *memory* conclude your development of the speech. Now it is time to get feedback from a peer.

Speech Criticism

As a speaker, when you open yourself to criticism, you have the opportunity to evaluate and improve your speaking skills (e.g., invention, organization, style, and delivery). As a listener, speech criticism tests your critical thinking skills because it includes both positive and negative comments. Feedback is offered with specific suggestions for improvement. Moreover, offering criticism tests your sensitivity as an interpersonal communicator.

Speech criticism includes two parts:

1. Judgments are a critic's opinion about the merits of the speech (e.g., "I liked your speech").
2. Reasons are statements that justify a critic's judgments (e.g., "I liked your speech because your sense of humor made me see this topic in a new way").

Receiving criticism from classmates about your speeches benefits you as a speaker. You are more likely to pay attention to criticisms that several people offer than to those offered by only one person. You are likely to accelerate your improvement as a speaker if you receive feedback from all members of your audience.

As a listener, follow these guidelines to become an effective and appropriate speech critic:

1. Begin with an "I" statement that explains what you liked about the speech.
2. Provide reasons for what you liked based on specific aspects of the speech (e.g., Content, Organization, and Delivery). Be as specific as possible. Saying "good delivery" is too vague. Saying, "you showed enthusiasm through your volume and gestures" is specific and tells the speaker what aspects of the delivery stood out to you as a listener.
3. Discuss any weaknesses you identify about specific aspects of the speech (e.g., Content, Organization, Delivery, and Media use). What can the speaker do next time to improve? Keep your criticisms constructive, but do not be afraid to offer suggestions for improvement. For example, if you said "your voice was a little soft. Try to project to the back of the room," you would be offering a specific, constructive critique.

What else can you do to become an effective and appropriate listener in a public communication setting? We discuss this in-depth in the next section.

AS A LISTENER, HOW DO I SUSTAIN AN ETHICS OF LISTENING?

Beard's (2009) choices for an ethics of listening, discussed in Chapter 1, help you discover how to become an appropriate and effective listener in a public communication environment. What can you do to be actively involved in the interaction?

Listening Behaviors

First, in order to move away from listening selectively, you need to **find something of interest** (Brommelje, 2013). Making connections between what you are listening to and your life experiences will help you stay focused. Imhof (2001) called these behaviors *interest management strategies*—ways to help listeners reach desirable personal outcomes. They included, "more comprehensive understanding, deeper level processing, more reflective assessment of new material, integration of new information into existing knowledge structures, and improved processing characteristics (e.g., sustaining attention and selective focus, better retention)" (p. 16). Consider, for example, how learning to summarize business cases in an introduction to business class could

EFFECTIVE LISTENING BEHAVIORS
- Find something of interest to you
- Focus your attention and attend to main points
- Take notes
- Minimize distractions (e.g., put away cell phones)
- Repeat main ideas silently
- Withhold judgment

help you train a new employee at your campus job because you know how to summarize the most important points concisely.

Second, Brownell (2013) proposed that we can improve immediate memory, and, consequently, listening skills, if we **focus attention** and **attend to the main points** (pp. 142–143). Moreover, we can develop the following habits to direct attention: **take notes** and **minimize distractions** (Bommelje, 2013). We may be reluctant to power down cell phones and other digital media during our interactions with others (e.g., class and meetings), but we may enjoy this "media fast." Some of us may even appreciate an excuse not to check Facebook and respond to texts.

Third, with this newfound freedom, you can improve short-term memory by using the extra time between the number of words the speaker can say (150 words a minute) and the number of words you can comprehend (600 words a minute). We recommend using this "space" time, now that you know you have it, to **repeat main ideas** silently in your mind. Brownell (2013) explained how repetition and the ability to **chunk material** or "grouping items so that you have fewer to remember" (p. 144) build short-term memory, which is needed to recall information in the future.

Finally, when arriving at the decision to listen together, both Imhof (2001) and Brommelje (2012) advocated for listeners to **withhold judgment** by noting emotional triggers. For example, when someone states the opposite political opinion from yours, recognize that your immediate response is to counter the argument. Naming "partisan politics" as an emotional trigger will remind you to seek first to understand, and not to justify your opinion.

Conclusion

In this chapter, we explored how to develop a listener-centered persuasive presentation by analyzing the audience and situation and using the five canons of rhetoric: invention, arrangement, style, delivery, and memory. We discovered that a persuasive argument includes both an assertion and support, along with valid forms of reasoning.

Consequently, when learning about *invention*, we discovered how to reason from definition, sign, cause, generalization, and analogy. Moreover, we avoided logical fallacies such as post hoc and slippery slope for cause reasoning; sweeping and hasty generalizations for generalization reasoning; and ad hominem and ad populum for diversions from main ideas.

When learning about *arrangement* and *style*, we focused on effective transitions and repetition, in addition to concrete and figurative language to help listeners engage with new material. We practiced effective and appropriate physical *delivery*, and emphasized nonverbal cues such as artifacts, kinesics, and presentational aids. We also discussed vocalics and the need to pay attention to volume, rate, and articulation.

Finally, we explored how to sustain an ethics of listening in a public communication context. We learned a number of listening behaviors (e.g., find something of interest, take notes, and withhold judgment) to help create meaning together. Now, we are ready to transfer these important communication skills to an interpersonal context.

REFERENCES

Adams, W. C., and Cox, E. S. 2010. The teaching of listening as an integral part of an oral activity: an examination of public-speaking texts. *International Journal of Listening* 24:89–105. DOI:10.1080/10904011003744524

Aristotle. 1990. Rhetoric. In *The rhetorical tradition: readings from classical times to the present*, ed. P. Bizzell and B. Herzberg, 151–94. Boston, MA: Bedford Books. Original printing 1909.

Beard, D. 2009. A broader understanding of the ethics of listening: Philosophy, cultural studies, media studies and the ethical listening subject. *International Journal of Listening* 23:7–20. DOI:10.1080/10904010802591771

Bommelje, R. 2013. *Listening pays: achieve significance thorough the power of listening.* Orlando, FL: Leadership & Listening Institute.

Brownell, J. 2013. *Listening: attitudes, principles, and skills.* New York: Pearson.

Burke, K. 1969. *A grammar of motives.* Berkeley: University of California Press.

California State University, Chico. 2010. *Evaluating information—applying the CRAAP test.* Retrieved from www.csuchico.edu/lins/handouts/eval_websites.pdf

Carman, G. 2006. *Rhetorical conquests: Cortes, Gomara, and renaissance imperialism.* Purdue studies in Romance literatures v. 35. West Lafayette, IN: Purdue University Press.

Cavender, N. M., and Kahane, H. 2013. *Logic and contemporary rhetoric: the use of reason in everyday life.* 12th ed. Stamford, CT: Cengage Learning.

Debord, G. 1983. *Society of the spectacle.* Detroit: Black & Red.

Fard, M. F. 2012, March 2. Sandra Fluke, Georgetown student called a 'slut' by Rush Limbaugh, speaks out. *Washington Post.* Retrieved from www.washingtonpost.com/blogs/the-buzz/post/rush-limbaugh-calls-georgetown-student-sandra-fluke-a-slut-for-advocating-contraception/2012/03/02/gIQAvjfSmR_blog.html

Haney, W. V. 1992. *Communication & interpersonal relations: texts and cases.* 6th ed. Boston, MA: Irwin.

Imhof, M. 2001. How to listen more efficiently: self-monitoring strategies in listening. *International Journal of Listening* 15:2–19. DOI:10.1080/1090 4018.2001.10499042

Lunceford, B. 2007. The science of orality: implications for rhetorical theory. *The review of communication* 7:83–102.

Morreale, S. P., Spitzberg, B. H., and Barge, J. K. 2007. *Human communication: motivation, knowledge, & skills.* 2nd ed. Belmont, CA: Thomson Wadsworth.

Ogden, C. K., and Richard, I. A. 1946. *The meaning of meaning: a study of the influence of language upon though and of the science of symbolism.* London: Routledge & Kegan Paul ltd.

School Vouchers Undermine Education. 1999, June 15. *Wilmington Morning Star,* 6A. http://news.google. com/newspapers?id=vXpaAAAAIBAJ&sjid=1R4EAAAAIBAJ&pg=6146%2C6007775

CHAPTER 3
INTERPERSONAL COMMUNICATION

LEARNING OBJECTIVES

By the end of this chapter, you should be able to:

- Explain how to create supportive interpersonal communication climates.
- Tie the elements of supportive climates to mediated communication.
- Describe how ethical listening behaviors and nonverbal cues impact interpersonal communication.
- Explain key interpersonal communication skill clusters: coordination, composure, expressiveness, and attentiveness.
- Be descriptive and paraphrase to demonstrate attentiveness.
- Introduce new topics and ask follow-up questions to demonstrate coordination.
- Use good posture and employ an empathic assertion to demonstrate composure.
- Make eye contact and use vocal variety to demonstrate expressiveness.

WHAT COMMUNICATION SKILLS TRANSFER FROM PUBLIC TO INTERPERSONAL COMMUNICATION SETTINGS?

Interpersonal communication—one-to-one interaction—involves many of the same communication skills developed for persuasive speaking settings: ethical listening behaviors, appropriate language and nonverbal cues, and reasoned arguments. In this chapter, we build upon these foundational skills and add a new setting, the workplace, in

38 Chapter 3 Interpersonal Communication

which to think about communication competence. Because 90% of what happens in an organization has nothing to do with formal events, most workplace communication involves informal interactions (Andrews & Baird, 2005, p. 70). We contend that if you first understand and then implement *effective* interpersonal communication behaviors, you will become a more *appropriate* interpersonal communicator at work, exhibiting "principled, productive, and compassionate life that improves the human condition" (Manchester University, 2013, para. 1).

Does an appeal to become a competent communicator in the workplace have *salience* for you? Does it motivate you to read further? What other motivators do you suggest: Building a career? Making a difference in a community organization? Once you determine what motivates you to read further, consider the outcomes of your efforts: you will recognize the difference between supportive and defensive climates, and will be able to supportively communicate with others.

HOW DO LISTENING, LANGUAGE, AND NONVERBAL COMMUNICATION WORK TOGETHER TO BUILD SUPPORTIVE COMMUNICATION CLIMATES?

Supportive Communication Climates

Communication expert Jack Gibb (1961) discovered that when we perceive a threat, we expend a great deal of time defending ourselves, our egos. These defensive behaviors correlate positively with losses in communication efficiency, and thus create **defensive climates**—negative communication environments. Gibb spent eight years recording discussions in various work settings, so his research is cited in communication textbooks and used in the workplace. He identified six characteristics of supportive communication climates, and juxtaposed them with the characteristics of defensive communication climates. Lahman (2001) created a handout with key words to help students and employees distinguish between defensive characteristics and their supportive counterparts (Table 3.1).

Gibb (1961) found that these six sets of characteristics interact. If a communicator regards someone as equal, open, and spontaneous, then an evaluative message is neutralized, and it may not even be perceived (p. 143). He also included *nonverbal cues* in his explanation of defensive climates (e.g., negative tone of voice), in addition to cues that indicate concern and understanding (e.g., leaning forward). In order to continue to build a communicative perspective, let us plan how to use supportive statements when faced with difficult interactions.

Description versus Evaluation

Descriptive statements include specific behaviors and actions, whereas evaluative statements contain judgment and blame. For example, if you disagree with a professor about a grade and exclaim, "Your criteria are unclear," you have made an *evaluative statement*. Your proclamation might provoke a defensive response from a professor who spent hours creating the assignment and years researching the concepts.

Creating Positive Communication Climates

Defensive Climate	Problems Created	Supportive Climate
1. EVALUATION: Judge or blame.	→ Feeling judged increases our defensiveness	1. DESCRIPTION: Request information.
2. CONTROL: Impose values & solutions.	→ We resist someone trying to control us.	2. PROBLEM ORIENTATION Collaborate to define & solve problem.
3. STRATEGY: Deceive with gimmicks & maneuvers.	→ If we perceive strategy, we become defensive.	3. SPONTANEITY: Be straightforward and honest.
4. Neutrality: Demonstrate lack of concern.	→ If other lack concern, we become defensive.	4. EMPATHY Identify with feelings and emotions.
5. SUPERIORITY: Show power, position, wealth, etc.	→ Superior actions arouse our defensiveness.	5. EQUALITY Demonstrate mutual respect and trust.
6. CERTAINTY: Know all the answers & need to win.	→ "Know-it-alls" arouse our defensiveness.	6. PROVISIONALISM Experiment and explore options.

*ADAPTED FROM JACK R. GIBB, "DEFENSIVE COMMUNICATION," JOURNAL OF COMMUNICATION, 1961.

Table 3.1 Supportive Communication Climates Handout.

To be *descriptive* in this situation, you could respond with "I-statements" that take responsibility for your unique perspective of the assignment, and which might be different from others' perspectives. Then follow your "I-statements" with a request for information about a specific part of the assignment. In this situation, saying, "I do not know what you mean by key words on note cards. Can you help me understand what you mean?'" is descriptive.

Similarly, in the workplace, if you evaluate a colleague with the following statement, "The rough draft of the report you turned in is sloppy," you may create a defensive climate. Instead, begin with an "I-statement" and request more information: "I think that the wording in the first two paragraphs could include more client-specific language. What ideas do you have for words that would resonate with our client?"

Problem Orientation versus Control

When you have a problem orientation, you collaborate to define and solve a problem. On the other hand, if you exhibit control, you focus on what you think is best. A control statement can involve threatening others or making ad hominem attacks, whereas a problem orientation focuses on answers and solutions that benefit everyone and that satisfy objectives.

In the same disagreement with a professor, you might begin sentences with "we" and provide ideas to solve the problem. For example, to demonstrate a *problem orientation* instead of *control*, you might ask, "Can we identify words together, so that I understand what you mean by key words?" When others hear the word "we," they are included in the dialogue and feel respected.

In an argument with a colleague, you might create a defensive climate if you say the following in an exasperated voice, "What did you *do* to my computer software?" Hopefully, you will remember how to create a supportive climate and demonstrate a problem orientation, "Let's work together to figure out what happened with our software."

Spontaneity versus Strategy

Spontaneity involves being open and honest with others. Strategy, in Gibb's usage, involves manipulating others or having some sort of hidden agenda. It means focusing on your own goals but keeping them from others. To be *spontaneous* instead of *strategic*, you might express curiosity when speaking to your professor about your speech by saying, "I wonder if it would help for us to write one note card together." Such spontaneity keeps both people focused on the task at hand.

In a future work environment, you and your colleagues may feel like manipulating a low-performing colleague with a bribe: "If you stay late and take work home, I bet our manager will notice and give you a raise, and we will be able to finish our report." Instead of thinking only about your own goals, you could be curious about what is keeping him or her from completing the task at hand. You may find that personal situations at home require all of his or her spare time and energy.

Empathy versus Neutrality

The most difficult characteristic of a supportive climate to demonstrate is *empathy*. Empathy is being helpful and expressing concern for others. It is juxtaposed with *neutrality* because Gibb (1961) found people do not like to be ignored; it makes them feel disregarded and irrelevant. Neutrality lacks the caring aspect of ethical communication. It makes others feel they are unimportant.

Consequently, demonstrating genuine concern requires careful listening. Some people dislike phrases such as "I know how you feel" and questions like "how does that make you feel?" These attempts at empathy can seem contrived. However, honest efforts to understand how others feel begin with tentative phrases such as "I think you *might* be feeling frustrated." Expressing your concern allows other people to confirm how they feel, and encourages them to explore and change their feelings.

One aspect of nonverbal communication that can be used to show empathy is **haptics**, or the use of touch. We can use touch to communicate power, support, and affection. Consider the various contexts in which we give or receive hugs, offer handshakes or high-fives, or hold hands. However, touch must be used carefully, as individuals have different tolerance levels and interpretations for touch. Cultural differences are also important. While putting your hand on someone's shoulder might be intended to communicate supportiveness, the person being touched could interpret it negatively. Do not assume that others want to be hugged—ask first if you are unsure.

Equality versus Superiority

Equality means each person has an opportunity to speak his or her mind, and respects others. Superiority is closely related to control, but in this context is more focused on an individual's attitude in relational contexts. Superiority is about having a sense of entitlement over others or feeling that, for some reason, you are better than they are. You could feel this way without actually attempting to take control over the situation or threatening others; you could express *superiority* by leaving out someone you dislike.

In the ongoing example, the professor may have more power than the student, but the student can respond in ways that respect the professor's expertise. For example, if you are the student, you could ask, "How should we handle our disagreement about criteria?" This question encourages equality by respecting the expertise of one person and the willingness to learn of the other. Similarly, in the example with the low-performing employee at work, you could brainstorm with your colleague about completing work in a timely manner, in light of little time and energy.

> What characteristics would you add to Gibb's (1961) six interactive sets? Add sentence "starters" to the ones we provide:
> - *Description:*
>   I find _____
>   (I + SPECIFIC BEHAVIORS)
> - *Problem orientation:*
>   We can _____
>   (WE + IDEAS),
> - *Spontaneity:*
>   I wonder if _____
>   (I + WONDER/CURIOSITY)
> - *Empathy:*
>   I think you might be feeling _____
>   (I + THINK YOU MIGHT BE FEELING)

Provisionalism versus Certainty

Provisionalism focuses on hearing and exploring all ideas. It requires you to forego championing one idea so that you can entertain others. It also encourages you to consider everyone's contributions. In contrast, certainty means you are sure you know all the answers. Certainty is about winning an argument or just refusing to acknowledge that other points of view could be correct. It is important to value the contributions of others. In this case you are not taking sides, but are instead trying to summarize and open the channels for other ideas.

Even though *certainty* seems similar to control, you could try to take control of a situation without thinking that you know everything there is to know. In the professor-student interaction example, you could express *provisionalism* by saying "I realize there are things about the criteria I may not understand. Can you help explain them to me?"

Now that you can explain the six sets of characteristics, let us explore more recent conclusions about Gibb's (1961) work. Researchers have shown that the characteristics may actually be separated into "task" and "people" functions. For example, colleagues who use *description* and *problem orientation* focus on individuals involved in an interaction, taking good care of people. Those who exhibit *empathy* and *spontaneity*, as well as *equality* and *provisionalism*, are viewed as collaborative because they focus on completing tasks (Forward, Czech, & Lee, 2011). On the other hand, colleagues who use statements that *involve control, certainty,* and *superiority* are perceived as authoritarian when completing tasks, and those who use *strategic* and *neutral* messages are considered manipulative in their regard for others (Forward et al., 2011).

What are the implications of these findings for supportive communication climates? These findings underscore the importance of the *relational* (people) and *content* (subject matter) functions in interpersonal messages. Cooper (as cited in Trenholm & Jensen, 2013) proposed that communicators have two important responsibilities in interpersonal interactions. First, they must be able to complete cognitive tasks such as separating facts from opinions, analyzing the content of messages, and recalling details of a conversation. Second, they must be able to accomplish relational tasks; they must indicate involvement, make the other person comfortable, and show support. (p. 110). How does it change your interactions to know that each interpersonal message has both content and relational components? Perhaps this new knowledge makes sense to you because you often take the advice of a good friend over that of a parent, even when the content of the message is the same. With this fresh understanding, we explore how an ethical approach to listening impacts supportive communication climates.

> **SUPPORTIVE CLIMATES AND MEDIATED COMMUNICATION**
>
> Contributing to a supportive communication climate can be particularly difficult through text messages, Facebook updates, and Tweets, and even through phone calls. We can easily make context errors, fail to account for cultural differences, and forget that we cannot control the meanings of our words.
>
> Moreover, mediated communication can at times seem designed to encourage us to defend our egos (and ourselves). The relative anonymity of some online environments can contribute to uses of strategy, neutrality, and evaluation. We can even misinterpret empathy in text messages, because it relies heavily on nonverbal cues such as gesture and tone of voice (Knapp, Hall, and Horgan, 2013).
>
> Nevertheless, many professions use mediated communication to build supportive climates. Health care providers, pharmacists, educators, and social workers are just some of the professionals working to construct descriptive, problem-oriented, spontaneous, empathic, equal, and provisional communication online.

Listening and Supportive Climates

Consider the impact of an ethics of listening when creating supportive communication climates. For example, in Chapter 1, you recognized that listening to the other person helped you create meaning (Shotter, 2009). Being descriptive, using a problem orientation, and taking good care of the people in the interaction fulfill this ethical imperative.

In Chapter 2, you refined specific listening behaviors, such as finding something of interest, focusing attention, attending to main ideas, taking notes, minimizing distractions, repeating ideas, and withholding judgment, so that you could focus on the speaker's message. These behaviors demonstrate empathy and spontaneity. What other listening behaviors do you use in the classroom, or in other public communication contexts, that might transfer to interpersonal settings? Which ones encourage supportive communication climates?

We find that *reframing*—finding a new angle from which to view a topic and speaker—is another important behavior proposed by Imhof (2001). Because listening and reframing behaviors help sustain attention, they improve retention of information in interpersonal communication, as well as in public speaking (e.g., they help us recognize the relevance of a topic and temporarily set aside negative feelings toward a topic). More importantly, when we find a new perspective, we demonstrate respect for a person in the present moment, and we provide the space and time to create meaning.

To help assess the appropriateness and effectiveness of interpersonal listening behaviors in supportive climates, Wolvin and Cohen (2012) proposed that listening includes contextual and ethical assessments, as well as cognitive, affective, and behavioral evaluations. We have learned all of these dimensions in previous chapters:

- **Cognitive:** "I understand how complex the listening process is and that there are multiple ways of listening and processing information" (i.e., the listening process includes receiving, constructing meaning, and responding).
- **Affective:** "I am more aware of my emotional barriers I experience in listening" (i.e., withhold judgment by knowing emotional triggers).
- **Behavioral:** "I keep focused on the speaker so I can listen to their whole message" (i.e., find something of interest, attend to main ideas, repeat ideas silently, and minimize distractions).
- **Contextual:** "I am aware of what settings I'm in and use different skills to better listen in them" (i.e., appreciative, comprehensive, critical, and empathetic)
- **Ethical:** "I work harder to not make immediate judgments about a message but rather listen to the arguments and then evaluate them" (i.e., the choices to create an ethics of listening) (Wolvin & Cohen, 2012, p. 66)

Nonverbal Cues Across Cultures

Hall (1959) called nonverbal communication the "silent language," when he first called attention to cultural differences in nonverbal codes. He drew on his experience training foreign-service workers to advocate appropriate and effective cross-cultural communication.

The following examples illustrate the poignant impact of culture (values and behaviors) on nonverbal communication:

1. [North] Americans in Greece were unable to conclude agreements needed to start new projects. . . . First, [North] Americans pride themselves on being outspoken and forthright. The Greeks regard these qualities as a liability. They are taken to indicate a lack of finesse, which the Greeks deplore. The [North] American directness immediately prejudiced the Greeks. Second, when the [North] Americans arranged meetings with the Greeks they tried to limit the length of the meetings and to reach agreements on general principles first, delegating the drafting of details to subcommittees. The Greeks regard this practice as a device to pull the wool over their eyes. The Greek practice is to work out details in front of all concerned and continue meetings for as long as is necessary. (p. 15)
2. In Latin America the interaction distance is much less than it is in the United States. Indeed, people cannot talk comfortably with one another unless they are very close to the distance that evokes either sexual or hostile feelings in the North American. The result is that when [the Latin Americans] move close, [North Americans] withdraw and back away. As a consequence, [Latin Americans] think [North Americans] are distant or cold, withdrawn and unfriendly . . . [North Americans] who have spent time in Latin America without learning these space considerations make other adaptations, like barricading themselves behind their desks, using chairs and [computer] tables to keep the Latin American at what is to [the North American] a comfortable distance. The result is that the Latin American may even climb over the obstacles until he has achieved a distance at which he can comfortably talk. (p. 209)

What do we learn about the culture-specific use of *time* in Example 1? About *space* in Example 2? Hall (1959) introduced the term **monochronic** (doing one thing at a time) to explain how people in the United States use time: American business people value punctuality; they begin meetings on time so that they can be finished quickly and move on to the next task (p. 178). He contrasted monochromic cultures with **polychronic** (doing many things at once) cultures, where people are less schedule-driven and value relationships (p. 173).

Hall (1959) originated the study of **proxemics**—the varying distances at which people feel comfortable communicating face-to-face. You might have learned about proxemics when someone told you to "back off" because you were invading his or her "personal bubble." Perhaps you have issued this warning as well. Hall (1966) delineated four distances available for communication: *intimate* (0 to 18 inches), *personal* (18 inches to 4 feet), *social* (4 to 12 feet), and *public* (12 feet and beyond). In the United States, people invite few people into their intimate spaces. Do you feel comfortable standing toe-to-toe with a stranger? Perhaps now you understand why people stare straight ahead and look up in elevators in the United States; other people are too close for comfort.

> **PROXEMICS AND ENVIRONMENT**
>
> As part of the study of space, proxemics also includes the environment and spatial arrangement in nonverbal communication. Think about the difference between a classroom setup in rows and a classroom setup in a circle. What expectations do you have about each class based on the way the room is arranged? The way that we arrange spaces facilitates certain types of interaction.

How does knowledge of nonverbal codes and proxemics affect your interactions with people from other cultures? With friends who use *time* and *space* differently than you? Hall (1959) proposed that you do not have to leave your country to encounter differences: "There are differences between families and differences between men and women; occupational differences, status differences, and regional differences" (p. 183). Differences are interesting to explore, and differences can cause conflict. What do we do when our differences escalate into conflict?

WHAT INTERPERSONAL SKILLS WILL HELP TRANSFORM INTERPERSONAL CONFLICT?

Interpersonal conflict occurs when two people in a relationship disagree; they see their "goals as incompatible" (Trenholm & Jensen, 2013, p. 117). This means that one or both persons may feel the other person is not being *appropriate*, while both are trying to reach their goals (*effectiveness*). Morreale, Spitzberg, and Barge (2007) proposed that one of the reasons conflict is so difficult to manage is because it "pits key competence dimensions against one another . . . to the extent that the other person is effective, you are likely to be ineffective" (p. 194). How do we use what we have learned about supportive communication behaviors to transform these conflicts?

We propose that supportive climate characteristics, when combined with ethical listening skills and nonverbal cues, provide the specific communication behaviors needed to remember the four "general-level skills" outlined by Spitzberg and Cupach (as cited in Morreale et al., 2007, p. 189). Spitzberg and Cupach clustered 100 interpersonal skills into four basic skill clusters:

1. **Attentiveness:** displaying concern for, interest in, and attention to the other person or persons in the interaction.
2. **Coordination:** displaying deft management of timing, initiation and closure of conversations, topic management, and so on.
3. **Composure:** displaying assertiveness, confidence, being in control.
4. **Expressiveness:** displaying vividness and animation in verbal and nonverbal expression (as cited in Spitzberg, 2006, p. 638).

To demonstrate these interpersonal *skills* clusters, we explain each one and provide examples. We use a disagreement between a student and a coach to illustrate the behaviors needed in each cluster.

Attentiveness

The supportive climate characteristic of *description*, in tandem with the listening skill of **paraphrasing** (summarizing content and feelings), helps you remain attentive to another person. In the heat of the moment, others need to know that you listen with concern, that you acknowledge and respect strong feelings. When you attempt to be descriptive and include paraphrases, you stay in the present moment; you might even resist pulling in past disagreements.

For example, in a conflict with a coach about sprint workouts, a student created the following response after the coach insisted that sprint workouts would help the student to work on speed (she needed speed to have a successful jump): "I understand the sprint workouts will help me with my speed and help me obtain a successful jump (*paraphrase*). How can we enhance my speed without doing 200-meter runs (*description*) that limit my ability to perform?"

This example highlights the need to plan what you might say when involved in a difficult dialogue. Similarly, you may find that supportive climate characteristics are not mutually exclusive. For example, *description* phrases quickly become *problem orientation* statements with the addition of "we" and a new idea for potential agreement.

Coordination

The supportive climate characteristic, *problem orientation*, combined with the listening skill, **clarifying questions** (follow-up questions we ask to explore another's perspective.) helps you coordinate interpersonal interactions. In conflict situations, we often forget to brainstorm for solutions. Because we are often overcome with anger, some conflict resolution experts suggest counting to 10 before trying to respond.

In addition to remembering to breathe, we suggest beginning sentences with "we" and thinking of as many ideas as you can, perhaps combining solutions you thought were "either-or" and "both-and." In our student-coach example, saying "we can use the 200-meter sprints and include more instruction on jumping" uses coordination. You will be surprised how frequently great solutions require you to combine ideas.

Finally, suggesting new ideas (*problem orientation*) tempers anger. When you are busy with *paraphrases* and *descriptions*, as detailed above, your attentiveness spurs creative problem solving. When students have a problem orientation, they are often surprised by how many options they can find to resolve roommate disagreements and frustrations with professors.

Composure

This skill cluster involves maintaining good *posture* for competent interpersonal communication. You might also recognize this nonverbal behavior as one you demonstrated in a public speaking context. In addition, composure requires you to be assertive and express *empathy*. Morreale et al. (2007) contended that the "most competent form [of composure] is empathic assertion, the attempt to recognize and grant legitimacy to others in a situation while simultaneously expressing your own right or views" (p. 193).

As we discussed earlier in this chapter, *empathy* might be the most difficult supportive climate characteristics to demonstrate. Students often include the phrase, "I feel that," and confuse expressing their own feelings with acknowledging another's feelings first. Stephen Covey (2004) argued for "seeking first to understand, then to be understood when we listen with the intent to understand others" (p. 153). Listening to understand means empathizing with another, and not focusing on who is right and who is to blame.

In our student-coach example, the student begins the interaction with *empathy* by acknowledging the coach's feelings: "I think you have a lot on your mind with the upcoming meet, so you might feel frustrated when a student approaches you with individual concerns at this point in your day." Although students admit these interactions feel contrived in the planning stages, when they rehearse the lines and hear others rehearse the lines, these supportive characteristics often surface in conversations with peers when they are not discussing interpersonal role plays. *Repetition* works in interpersonal settings, much like it does in public ones.

Expressiveness

This skill cluster involves *nonverbal cues*. We suggest two, *vocal variety* and *eye contact*, because you are familiar with and have demonstrated both of these in a public speaking context. How did you practice these important skills? What did you learn from your peers about what makes these skills both *appropriate* and *effective* in public speaking contexts? How will this knowledge transfer to interpersonal interactions?

We found in public speaking contexts that when we are enthusiastic about a topic, others follow—vocal variety is contagious. If you are monotone and uninterested, then others will be lethargic as well. In an interpersonal context, enthusiasm works the same way. Similarly, when we are genuinely concerned about a topic and a person, and that concern is exhibited through a soothing vocal tone, others feel consoled.

In the United States, eye contact indicates we care about another. Looking into another person's eyes confirms their humanity, and respect is forthcoming. In conflict situations, we have to be careful not to "stare down" the other person, which indicates a desire to control and an unwillingness to collaborate. Similarly, in other cultures, direct eye contact is a sign of disrespect. As we discussed earlier in this chapter, *nonverbal cues* are culturally situated and we must understand the cultural context within which we are communicating.

Conclusion

In this chapter, we gained knowledge about how to create supportive interpersonal communication climates with specific *description, problem orientation, spontaneity, empathy, equality* and *provisionalism* behaviors. We also considered how these climate characteristics translate to mediated communication, such as texting and social media. These important supportive communication behaviors work in tandem with ethical listening behaviors and *nonverbal cues* to demonstrate four important interpersonal communication skill clusters: coordination, composure, expressiveness, and attentiveness.

In order to demonstrate attentiveness, we learned to be descriptive and to paraphrase, and to use good posture and empathic assertion when exhibiting composure. We explored how to propose ideas for a problem orientation and ask clarifying questions to show coordination, in addition to making eye contact and using vocal variety, important nonverbal cues, to demonstrate expressiveness. Now, we are ready to transfer these important communication skills to the final context we will explore in this book: small group communication.

REFERENCES

Andrews, P. H., and Baird, J. E. (2005). *Communication for business and the professions.* 8th ed. Long Grove, IL: Waveland Press.

Covey, S. R. 2004. *The 8th habit: from effectiveness to greatness.* New York: Franklin Covey.

Forward, G. L., Czech, K., and Lee, C. M. 2011. Assessing Gibb's supportive and defensive communication climate: an examination of measurement and construct validity. *Communication Research Reports* 28:1–15. DOI:10.10 80/08824096.2011.541360

Gibb, J. R. 1961. Defensive communication. *Journal of Communication* 11:141–8. DOI:10.1111/j.1460-2466.1961.tb00344.x

Hall, E. T. 1959. *The silent language.* Greenwich, CT: Fawcett.

Hall, E. T. 1966. *The hidden dimension.* Garden City, NY: Doubleday.

Imhof, M. 2001. How to listen more efficiently: self-monitoring strategies in listening. *International Journal of Listening* 15:2–19. DOI:10.1080/1090 4018.2001.10499042

Knapp, M. L., Hall, J. A., and Horgan, T. G. 2013. *Nonverbal communication in human interaction.* 8th ed. Boston, MA: Wadsworth.

Lahman, M. P. 2001. Operationalizing supportive/defensive climates for undergraduates. *Communication Teacher* 15:13–4.

Manchester University. 2013. *Mission Statement.* Retrieved from Manchester University, North Manchester website: www.manchester.edu/Common/AboutManchester/mission.htm

Morreale, S. P., Spitzberg, B. H., and Barge, J. K. 2007. *Human communication: motivation, knowledge, & skills.* 2nd ed. Belmont, CA: Thomson Wadsworth.

Shotter, J. 2009. Listening in a way that recognizes/realizes the world of "the other." *International Journal of Listening* 23:21–43. DOI:10.1080/10904010802591904

Spitzberg, B. H. 2006. Preliminary development of a model and measure of computer-mediated communication (CMC) competence. *Journal of Computer-Mediated Communication* 11:629–66. Retrieved from http://jcmc.indiana.edu/

Trenholm, S., and Jensen, A. 2013. *Interpersonal communication.* 7th ed. New York: Oxford University Press.

Wolvin, A. D., and Cohen, S. D. 2012. An inventory of listening competency dimensions. *International Journal of Listening* 26:64–6. DOI: 10.1080/10904018.2012.677665

CHAPTER 4
SMALL GROUP COMMUNICATION

LEARNING OBJECTIVES

By the end of this chapter, you should be able to:

- Explain the key characteristics of a small group.
- List and describe the four phases of group development.
- Explain how task and relational roles influence a group's interaction and effectiveness.
- Lead and participate in group meetings by creating agendas and minutes.
- Participate in group decision-making techniques and address challenges.
- Describe how group leadership influences a group's interaction and effectiveness.
- Identify types of group conflict and when to use appropriate conflict management styles.

WHAT DO YOU LIKE ABOUT WORKING IN SMALL GROUPS?

Think about all of the groups you enjoy: clubs, sports teams, class groups, work groups, and service or church groups may come to mind. You also have family and friendship groups. What makes a group work well?

Groups vary in size, purpose, and duration, but they also share unique characteristics. In this chapter, we focus on work-based groups, although many of the skills we discuss can be applied to all groups. Small group competence—and the ability to work well in groups—is an important part of your education and your professional life. Even if you prefer to work alone, many of your classes and future employers will require group collaboration.

According to a 2012 study by the consulting firm Millennial Branding (Schawbel, 2012), 98% of employers want you to have effective oral and written communication skills for an entry-level position, and 92% find it very important that you have strong teamwork skills. As you may have learned in previous group experiences, teamwork skills are not always intuitive.

Whether you enjoy group work or you have some apprehension about it, you will explore the skills needed to manage group experiences, and you will add these skills to the listening and speaking skills you developed in public speaking and interpersonal communication activities. The purpose of this chapter is to explore what is unique about small group communication and learn how to manage group meetings, make group decisions, and handle group conflicts.

Key Characteristics of a Small Group

What makes a small group a small group? Many of us would say that size does, but small groups have additional characteristics. A group is not the same as a grouping or a more general collection or gathering of people (Keyton, 2006); small groups require shared goals and interdependence. For our purposes, we define a ***small group*** as "three or more people working interdependently for the purpose of accomplishing a task" (Myers & Anderson, 2008, p. 7). Small groups have three key features: group size, interdependence, and shared identity.

Group Size: A small group needs at least three people, but it is important to distinguish between interpersonal and group contexts. Think about what happens when you add a third person to what was previously a pair—communication changes significantly. Two people may form a coalition against the other person or make decisions by majority vote. While a group needs at least 3 members, the upper limit of a small group varies. Some scholars draw the upper limit as high as 15 members (Socha, 1997), at which point groups tend to splinter.

Interdependence: *Interdependence* means, "any group member's behavior influences both group members' task behaviors and their relational behaviors" (Bertcher, cited in Myers & Anderson, 2008, p. 7). When a group has ***goal interdependence***, members rely on each other to complete the task; they share superordinate goals, which are too complex to be completed by one person (Keyton, 2006). Group members should share understanding of tasks and common goals. For instance, if some group members are invested in the project, but other group members just want a passing grade, the group needs to discuss and negotiate those expectations at the outset.

In addition to task or goal interdependence, groups also experience ***behavioral interdependence***; the language and nonverbal cues used affect other group members. If group members ignore each other and only focus on doing individual tasks, the group does not have interdependence. Interdependence is not the same as **dependence**, where individuals are in a subordinate position to other group members (Keyton, 2006), or where group members cannot work without being in the presence of each other (Myers & Anderson, 2008).

Shared Identity and Norms: A key feature of a small group is a perception of belonging to the group; members understand themselves as group members. This perception is based on **group identity**: the "psychological and/or physical boundaries that distinguish a group member from a non-group member (Myers & Anderson, 2008, p. 10). Examples of physical boundaries include how a group sits together in class and a sports team wears the same uniform group sits together in class, or sports team wears the same uniform. Groups also share a sense of inclusion and cohesion, a psychological bond. Team names and shared phrases lead to a sense of cohesion and shared identity. After a while, you may find that members of your group develop shared **norms**, expectations of behavior. These norms can be positive, such as everyone participating, or negative, when a group develops a norm of pulling out cell phones during group meetings.

> **SOCIAL LOAFING**
>
> Interdependence is an important and necessary criterion for small group communication, but it does have a downside: trusting and relying on other group members can be difficult. Perhaps you have encountered this in previous class groups; you know what happens when some members do not contribute much and rely on others to pull the weight. Group communication scholars call this *social loafing* (Latane, Williams, & Harkins, 1979). When the size of the group is larger than the task requires, some members may coast on the efforts of others. Clear communication about expectations and norms from the beginning of the group's interaction can help prevent social loafing.

Tuckman (1965) developed the first model for how small groups develop over time by examining existing research on groups. Each of these phases may be brief or long periods of time, depending on the group and task.

In the *forming* phase, group members may feel a combination of excitement and anxiety as they consider their fit with the team and how other group members will perform. In this first stage, it is important for group members to establish clear goals for the group and get to know one another to develop trust.

The second phase is *storming*, where frustrations or disagreements occur about the task, expectations, and roles. The group lacks unity. Group members may be concerned about the ability to meet goals and fulfill their expectations. Interpersonal conflicts may also emerge. While we sometimes see conflict as negative, this is an important part of the group's development; some conflict is necessary to push the group to perform better and make effective decisions.

The *norming* phase is where groups resolve issues and develop cohesion. Emerging from the storming stage means the group has overcome problems, and group members feel more comfortable expressing their thoughts and opinions. The group has a sense of shared identity and begins to think of themselves with a "we" orientation. Group members feel accepted and understand their roles and expectations.

The ***performing*** phase is when the group is fully engaged in the team's tasks. This is a phase of peak productivity. Members are likely to feel a sense of interdependence and shared responsibility, and are willing to help one another when needed. Commitment to the group and the task is high.

The final phase, ***adjourning***, indicates the dissolution of a group. In a class, this may come at the end of the semester when the project is complete. In the workplace, a group may work together for years before the group ends.

Each of these phases can take varying amounts of time, but they also may not be precisely sequential. Groups may regress through the phases at different times. For example, new tasks may mean a return to the storming phase. Adding new group members into an existing group may mean the group has to return to a forming phase as they figure out how to integrate the new members.

WHAT SKILLS WILL BE HELPFUL IN MANAGING GROUP MEETINGS?

Because groups are task-oriented, many of the *language* behaviors (e.g., supportive climate characteristics) and *nonverbal* messages (e.g., proxemics, kinesics, oculesics) are needed to meet group objectives and complete activities. These messages might include giving or asking for direction on tasks, reporting and requesting information, and coordinating group activity and time (Keyton, 2006). Planning meetings, assigning tasks, generating ideas, clarifying points, and reporting progress are all examples of **task communication**.

In addition to task communication, groups have **relational communication**—messages that build connections and relationships (Keyton, 2006). Relational messages can be positive or negative. Positive relational messages may include showing friendliness through a smile, asking how a group member is doing, reducing tension through telling a joke, and smoothing over group conflict. Negative relational messages may include expressing dislike, withdrawal, and exclusion. *Nonverbal cues*, such as turning away from a group member to continue a conversation or glaring when a group member walks in, are examples of negative relational messages. If such messages become part of a group's norms, they can interfere with the completion of a group's tasks.

Task and relational communication may seem distinct, but many interactions will have both task and relational messages. For example, you suggest a kickball tournament as a fundraiser for your team. Another group member smiles and replies, "That's a great idea! I love kickball!" You are discussing a task-related topic, but your group member's encouraging reaction also expresses a positive relationship. Likewise, if you make the same suggestion and another group member rolls his eyes and smirks, you also have relational communication.

Groups need to balance their task and relational needs. A task-focused group still needs to form relationships in order to have cohesiveness. Some work groups may be overly social and spend most of their time chatting, which can be good for relationships and bad for completing tasks. Each group may have a different purpose and different needs for task and relational communication.

Group Roles

You may notice that group members tend to fall into certain patterns of behavior: they may be task-centered, relationship-centered, or ego-centered (focused on themselves). Perhaps there is someone in the group who always returns the group to the task at hand and seeks the input of others. Another member may jump in to smooth disagreements. Even the social loafer who looks at his or her phone during the entire meeting plays a role, albeit a negative one.

Group roles are sets of behaviors that individuals perform (Morreale, Spitzberg, & Barge, 2007). Group roles are informal and unassigned, and all groups have them. Many group members perform multiple roles, and complete different roles at different times. Roles emerge through interaction with others in the group. A role in one setting might be inappropriate in another. Group roles fall into three general categories: task, relational, and ego-centered (Benne & Sheats, 2007).

Task Roles: Task roles help groups achieve their tasks and objectives. They help move the group along by facilitating and coordinating group activities and decision making. There are many possible roles here; the following are a few that you might find in your own groups.

- **Initiator:** Proposes new ideas or procedures or a new way of thinking about the problem.
- **Information seeker:** Requests clarification of facts and ideas raised during discussion.
- **Information giver:** Provides authoritative information, facts, and relevant experiences.
- **Elaborator/coordinator:** Gives examples and further develops given ideas and suggestions while pulling together the ideas of the group.
- **Energizer:** Motivates the group to continue working and to take action.
- **Recorder:** Writes down important parts of group discussions and makes a record of group decisions (Benne & Sheats, 2007).

Relational Roles: Relational roles help maintain a positive interpersonal climate. They are also called maintenance roles because they create and maintain group-centered behavior.

- **Encourager:** Supports the participation of others and praises the contributions of group members. Accepts the viewpoints of others.
- **Harmonizer:** Manages conflict and relieves tension.
- **Gatekeeper:** Encourages participation from others and manages the flow of conversation to keep all members involved.
- **Follower:** Acts as an audience and goes along with the ideas of others (Benne & Sheats, 2007).

Ego-Centered Roles: Ego-centered roles are also called individual roles, because they favor the individual to the detriment of the group. The presence of ego-centered roles in a group is an opportunity for reflection about what is going on in the group that allows these roles to emerge. It could be a lack of communication competence, low group discipline or morale, or confusion over the task (Benne & Sheats, 1948/2007). If a group allows individual roles to become norms, they create defensiveness and hurt the group's ability to effectively complete its tasks.

Looking through these roles, you can probably pick out several past group members who fulfilled them. You may have fulfilled some of them yourself. Sometimes members deliberately perform these roles, but often they are not aware of the impact of their behavior on others.

- **Dominator:** Takes over group discussions, manipulates others, interrupts, gives orders, and otherwise tries to assert authority.
- **Clown:** Attempts to distract others from the task through goofing off or being cynical; is generally uninvolved in the group's task.
- **Recognition seeker:** Desires praise from others, wants to take credit, and brags about personal accomplishments.
- **Blocker:** Rejects others' ideas without adequate justification and is sullen or oppositional during group discussions (Benne & Sheats, 2007).

Task, relational, and ego-centered roles connect not only to task and relational communication but also to how the group manages conflict and leadership. Before we discuss those facets of group communication, we need to address some practical skills (related to several task roles) to facilitate productive group meetings.

Managing Group Meetings

Many meetings feel pointless, because the goals of the meeting are not clear. You may have experienced this: you scheduled a group meeting to work on a project, but did not specify what group members were supposed to have done prior to the meeting or what the group would do during the meeting. As we have noted in previous chapters, a communicative perspective includes making a plan. For small group communication, a well-planned meeting will get accomplished in the same amount of time as a poorly planned meeting.

Before you schedule a meeting, decide if you must meet in person, or if the tasks can be handled over the phone or through online collaboration. In the workplace, you may find that meetings take place through conference calls and Skype. Even now, you may plan meetings using text messages or Facebook. If you do communicate electronically, programs like Google Docs and Dropbox allow you to share documents so that everyone can access and edit the most current version.

However, there are times when a face-to-face meeting is necessary. In order to run meetings effectively, group members need to create meeting agendas and take minutes.

Even if your meeting is online or over the phone, it is still important to have a clear agenda and minutes so everyone can follow along.

Agendas: An *agenda* is a list of topics that need to be covered at a meeting. Why are you meeting? For how long will you meet? Ideally, an agenda is distributed at least a day before a meeting—and someone in the group should take responsibility for planning and running each meeting. Agendas do not need to be complicated, but they ought to contain a few elements (Figure 4.1):

- Meeting start and stop times, location, and date
- Expected attendees
- Purpose
- Items for discussion
- Decision items
- Any preparations attendees need to do before the meeting (Keyton, 2006).

First, you need to know the purpose of the meeting. Your purpose will help you plan the appropriate time and place for the meeting, and will establish the items for discussion. A "get to know your other group members" meeting has a very different purpose than does a "prepare for the project presentation" meeting. What do you need to accomplish at this meeting, and who needs to be there?

You also need to decide not only when the meeting will start but also when it will end. Instead of saying "we are meeting at 8:00," say, "we are meeting from 8:00–9:00." If you set a time limit, group members can avoid scheduling conflicts and are less likely to

---

Small Group Meeting Agenda: Team Awesome
Meeting Details: Tuesday, November 6, 8–9 PM, Oakwood Lounge
Expected Attendees: All members
Purpose: To create a group contract and divide assignments for the group presentation

Items for discussion:
1. Creating a group contract—due 11/14
    - **Prior to meeting, all members should brainstorm at least one rule they would like to put in the contract to present for discussion.**
    - **Sarah: Please bring your laptop so we can record our guidelines at the meeting**
    - Generate a list of agreeable policies and sanctions.
2. Preparing for the group presentation
    - Clarifying the assignment guidelines
    - Dividing work and setting deadlines
        Please take a look at the assignment sheet and chapter pages concerning our topic prior to the meeting. Bring these items with you to the meeting.
        What are our strengths as group members? What interests do we have? Decide on how the task can be broken down into small parts—assign parts to individual members.

Figure 4.1 Small group meeting sample agenda

lose focus. As we learned in Chapter 3, adding specific details, or being *descriptive*, helps build supportive communication climates.

The most important part of the agenda is a clear list of the things the group needs to discuss at the meeting and a list of any decisions that the group needs to make during the meeting. These are not always the same thing; a group may generate ideas at one meeting, and make a decision at another. Even if you do not plan the meeting, review the agenda before the meeting to know what you need to prepare.

Minutes: Minutes do not refer to the actual minutes spent in a meeting. Instead, *minutes* are a written record of what happened during the meeting (Figure 4.2). They should detail:

- Who was there?
- What was discussed?
- What was decided?
- Who agreed to do what?
- What does the group plan to do next? (Keyton, 2006).

Taking minutes may seem tedious, but it is an important task for effective groups. The key information recorded includes what decisions the group made and who is

---

Small Group Meeting Minutes: Team Awesome
Meeting Details: Tuesday, November 6, 8–9 PM, Oakwood
Lounge Attendees: Sarah, Eddie, Dave, Sue, Marcie
Purpose: To create a group contract and divide assignments for the group presentation

Items for discussion and action items:
1. Creating a group contract—due 11/14
    - Each member brought a list of possible guidelines to the meeting for discussion. Topics included attendance at group meetings, policies for missing deadlines, and communication climate. All members must agree on the policies in the contract. The group contract was typed on Sarah's laptop.
    - Sarah will email the contract to all members and bring a copy to class on 11/14 for all members to sign.
2. Preparing for the group presentation
    - Dividing work and setting deadlines—Topic: Group Roles
        - Dave volunteered to cover task roles during the presentation. He will send out an outline of his discussion by 11/17.
        - Eddie volunteered to cover relational roles during the presentation. He will send out an outline of his discussion by 11/17.
        - Sue volunteered to show a film clip and lead a short discussion on the types of roles in that clip. She will send out the clip and her discussion questions by 11/17.
        - Marcie volunteered to create the group's PowerPoint. All speaker notes are due to her by 11/20 at 5 PM so she can create the slides.

Figure 4.2 Small group meeting sample minutes

responsible for taking action. Make sure that someone who was not at the meeting would have a clear idea of what happened at the meeting. Similarly, when you make assignments for who is going to do what in a group, be sure to assign someone to complete a task by specifying exactly what is to be done and when.

HOW DO GROUPS MAKE GOOD DECISIONS?

Think about the ways you have made decisions in previous groups, whether in a class group, a friendship group, or with your family. Does one person usually make a decision and the others go along with it? Do you vote and have majority rule? Do you try to get everyone to agree?

Groups make better decisions than individuals when a diversity of perspectives and knowledge is needed. However, many groups do not make decisions effectively when the problem is complex and there are many potential solutions, or when the group is facing time pressure. Groups make better decisions when they follow a systematic process called the "Standard Agenda," and they can implement change when they follow a systematic process called "Appreciative Inquiry."

The Standard Agenda for Decision Making

The ***Standard Agenda*** is based on the functional theory of decision making, which describes, step-by-step, what groups need to do to make effective decisions (Gouran, 1999). Those steps, in order, include: define the problem, analyze the problem, identify the criteria, generate solutions, and evaluate solutions (Wood, Phillips, & Pedersen, 1986). To help you understand these steps, we use the example of deciding to attend a college. Imagine that you and your family make this decision.

- **Define the problem:** The first step is to identify the problem and to discuss the problem and its causes. Make the problem as specific as possible and create a concise problem statement. There might be multiple, interconnected problems, and your group may not be able to work with all of them at once. In this instance, work with a simple, core problem. In the case of choosing a college, your core problem is not what you are going to do after high school; it is that you are unsure of which colleges to apply.
- **Analyze the Problem:** The second step is to analyze the problem. This requires research and data collection to assess the problem's size and potential impact, and to understand why it exists. Ask your fellow group members if you have all the information you need to make a good decision. What else might you need to know? Have you looked at the problem from multiple angles (e.g., Is it better to be close to home or farther way? What scholarships and financial aid are being offered?) Think of the problem's signs and causes. How might different groups understand this problem (e.g., parents, high school counselors, or university admissions counselors?)

- **Identify the Criteria:** Third, you need to identify criteria for the solution. Members must determine the criteria for solutions without jumping ahead to the solutions themselves. These criteria should reflect values and what is important to the group. For our college choice example, you might need an institution that has generous financial aid, small class sizes, and specialized majors. You might be willing to compromise on some criteria, but others are not negotiable. In our example, because you are making this list before visiting colleges, you will not waste time looking at places that do not meet your needs; these were your criteria for making a decision.
- **Generating Solutions or Alternatives:** The fourth step is to generate as many solutions and alternatives as possible. Your group needs to generate a number of solutions and not just stop at a solution it immediately likes. A good way to do this is to create a list of alternatives that group members freely add to and modify. Concerning college choice, your family may generate a number of solutions (e.g., college X, college Y, college Z).
- **Evaluating Solutions/Alternatives:** Finally, evaluate the solutions and select the best one. Use your criteria as a guide and remember to think about how the decision will affect others outside your group. Assess the positive and negative aspects of each solution. In the college choice process, your family may pick the university that meets the largest number of criteria.

Appreciative Inquiry as a Means of Organizational Change

While the Standard Agenda includes the important elements your group needs when making a decision, it is not the only systematic approach to group decision making. The ***Appreciative Inquiry*** (AI) approach is a method for organizational change that uses the strengths of all those in the group. This method is especially useful in long-term groups who implement complex changes and decisions. Appreciative Inquiry focuses on what is going well with a project, envisions what can make it even better, and corrals group members' strengths.

Appreciative Inquiry follows a process of the "4Ds" of Discover, Dream, Design, and Destiny (Cooperrider, Whitney, & Stavros, 2008), which are detailed below:

- **Discovery:** *What works?* In the first phase, group members discover what they do well. If group members are new to each other, they discuss previous experiences; if the group has been together for a while, members discuss particular events or moments in the current group. Individual group members are encouraged to identify what he or she did and what others did to contribute to successful projects (Conklin, 2009). In essence, discovery helps groups set expectations and goals. It helps them focus on what is going well, not on what might be going wrong.
- **Dream:** *What might be?* In the next phase, group members generate ideas. These ideas should be freely generated, and not criticized. Think of best-case scenarios, and be creative. Because it is hard for group members not to worry about whether an idea is realistic during this phase, outrageous ideas such as flying members to an

exotic location to complete the task must be stated at the outset (Lahman, 2012). Similarly, group members must have opportunities to be heard and to share ideas.
- **Design:** *How can it be?* The design phase is a period of discussion and reflection about the ideas that have been raised. Group members discuss options (again, they do not criticize ideas) and clarify ideas that are confusing. They consider which ideas could make the most impact. They look at the goals generated in the discovery phase and the ideas generated in the dream phase and think about how to put them together in a realistic way. Group members may vote on ideas to determine which ideas reflect shared goals.
- **Destiny:** *What will be?* In the final stage, group members consider how to put their idea(s) into action. They move from the "wants" to the "wills" (Conklin, 2009). Group members should discuss what they are willing to commit to and implement. Not all of the ideas may be put into action now, but they should not be abandoned if the group believes in them. Consider what resources are needed (resources could be information, time, money, commitment, etc.), and decide who will complete what tasks by when.

Challenges to Group Decision Making

Both of these methods are useful guides to group decision making. However, groups sometimes face challenges in the decision-making process that damage group members' relationships and encourage poor decisions. Two of the most common challenges are grouphate and groupthink.

Grouphate: *Grouphate* is a negative predisposition toward group work that causes people to dislike working in a group (Keyton & Frey, 2002). Grouphate is rooted in negative group experiences, and individuals can experience it in varying degrees. Grouphate can harm the entire group, and is associated with lower academic performance on group projects; students with positive attitudes toward group work have greater academic success on group projects (Freeman, 1996).

If someone on your team has grouphate, he or she might have low expectations of other group members. People with strong grouphate might feel that they will do a better job by themselves and that they are going to be worse off for working with others. These individuals can be frustrating to work with, because they become self-fulfilling prophets: they anticipate negative experiences, act accordingly, and spread negativity to the group. The best way to overcome grouphate is to have positive group experiences. Consequently, if you dislike working in groups, be aware of how your attitude affects your group.

Groupthink: Groupthink is a major challenge to group decision making, and it can occur without the group even being aware of it. *Groupthink* is "a mode of thinking that people engage in when they are deeply involved in a cohesive in-group, when the members' strivings for unanimity override their motivation to realistically appraise alternative courses of action" (Janis, 1982, p. 9). Groupthink occurs when group members establish a norm that makes consensus the highest priority and diminishes alternatives to their final decision (Janis, 1982).

In groupthink, the group gets along well, is very cohesive, and avoids talking about ethical and moral aspects of decisions because doing so might damage cohesiveness. The group sets criteria, but then limits solutions to those that will not weaken cohesiveness. Members may also feel that the group makes good decisions no matter what, and they may reject information that goes against the assumed course of action. If new, contrary information becomes available, it might be dismissed to protect group members.

Groupthink happens under three conditions (Janis, 1982):

- Illusion of invulnerability: Members feel the group is infallible, and enhancing shared identity takes priority over information or opinions that might damage cohesiveness.
- Insulated group: The group rejects information that goes against its preferred mindset or decision. The group is insulated and does not seek outside information or opinions.
- Pressure to conform: Members who disagree conform because of high-pressure, high-stress situations, strong leaders who push for particular courses of action, and fear of losing group identity. Members who silently disagree censor their opinions and help maintain an illusion of unanimity.

You might have been in groups with groupthink without even realizing it. Have you ever waited until the last minute to work on a group project, and then everyone agreed with the first idea that someone suggested? Your group did not have time to really consider alternative options, and so may not have made the best decision. On a more extreme scale, groupthink may be at play in clubs and groups that practice hazing. Even if some members believe that the behavior is wrong, they may not speak up because they are afraid of being ostracized by the group or of hurting group identity.

Preventing Groupthink

In your experiences, how have groups pressured dissenting members into agreement? Now that you know what groupthink is, do you feel like you were ever part of a group that experienced groupthink? How might a group prevent groupthink?

First, make sure that the group has time to discuss and brainstorm ideas. Hurrying the brainstorming process is common in school groups, but it may result in faulty decision making (Myers & Anderson, 2008). Your communicative behaviors can prevent groupthink: actively listen to all group members, do not interrupt, ask questions, and avoid being passive or "checking out" of discussions (Di Salvo, Nikkel, & Monroe, 1989).

Second, as you learned above, decision-making procedures can help you explore multiple options. The group should ask, "What else do we need to know to make a good decision?" It is also important that members take on the role of a **critical advisor** (also called a *devil's advocate*). The purpose of this role is to ask questions and consider the negative points to a potential decision, such as "Why might this not be a good idea?" or "How can we mitigate these risks?"

Group members can rotate the devil's advocate role, or they can assign all members to take it on and make critical questions and objections a priority (Janis, 1972). The goal of a critical advisor is to be critical of ideas, not of people. All group members must be willing to accept criticism of their ideas. Regularly assigning this role makes idea evaluation a natural part of group discussions. Effective group leadership can also prevent groupthink.

WHAT LEADERSHIP SKILLS DO YOU HAVE? WHICH ONES DO YOU WANT TO DEVELOP?

What does leadership mean to you? How would you define it? Are people born leaders, or can they develop the skills to be leaders? **Leadership**, in the context of small groups, refers to "a communication process that helps groups organize themselves to meet desired goals" (Morreale et al., 2007, p. 248).

Leadership is not a position or a title: it is based on actions and behaviors with and toward others. You may have a perception of leadership as one person who directs a group, but effective leadership is much more than that. Leadership can be performed by anyone in the group, not just by an appointed "leader." Moreover, being a leader does not mean doing all the work for a group; it means helping the group find ways to accomplish the work together. Leadership involves both task and relational skills. Managing conflict between group members can be just as important as delegating tasks.

Becoming a Leader

According to Hollander (1978), individuals become leaders in a number of ways:

- **Appointed:** Someone external to the group, such as a manager, appoints one member to be a leader. This is very common in workplace situations, but it does not mean the appointed person will be an effective leader. The group may be less inclined to follow an appointed leader, and the group may feel that this method is unfair. If the group performs poorly, the appointed leader may be blamed, and the person that appointed the leader may be blamed.
- **Elected by group members:** The leader who is elected by group members has a greater sense of responsibility to the group, and members also have a strong investment in following this person. If things do not work out in the group, the leader is likely to take the blame.
- **Emerges over time:** An emergent leader is most common in school groups. The leader emerges over time through interaction with group members, and without being appointed or elected. Members may assess who is leader-worthy based on their trustworthiness and sense of authority. Your communication style is important because those who are verbally and nonverbally engaged and supportive of others are likely to emerge as leaders. Other group members evaluate your leadership potential based on your communication. Group members who contribute first and most often are likely to become emergent leaders.

Leadership Styles

Scholars have theorized about leadership in different ways. Although the *trait* approach looks at the personal qualities a leader might possess, the *functional* approach understands that leadership is based on communicative behaviors (Barge, 1997). This means that leadership skills can be learned, because effective leadership is about behaviors and practices that help groups accomplish their tasks.

The *style* approach to leadership is based on the idea that leaders use different leadership styles that affect group outcomes (Lewin, Lippitt, & White, 1939). This early work did not take into account how various situations influence group leadership behaviors, but it did give a useful framework of three basic leadership styles: democratic, autocratic, and laissez-faire.

The democratic and autocratic styles are opposite ends of a continuum. Those who use a **democratic** style try to involve everyone in the decision-making process and to maintain positive relationships with all group members. Democratic leaders also avoid promoting one idea over others. **Autocratic** leadership is directive, and the leader takes on a guiding and instructing role. Autocratic leaders have more power and final say than do their democratic counterparts. On the extreme end, autocratic leaders can be aggressive and controlling.

Both of these styles may be appropriate at different times; for example, democratic styles may bring in more diverse viewpoints, but autocratic styles may be useful when decisions need to be made quickly (Morreale et al., 2007). Autocratic leaders can increase the likelihood of groupthink by promoting one decision or idea over others and by shutting down members who might criticize their ideas.

The third style is called **laissez-faire** (a French phrase that literally means "let them do") and is a hands-off approach to leadership. In this style, groups work independently and leaders step in to assist as requested. Leaders trust groups to complete the work and do not often change roles.

You may find that your personal leadership preference is a blend of these styles, or that you adopt different styles in different situations. Depending on your familiarity with group members, familiarity with tasks, and external factors such as deadlines and work environments, you may adapt your leadership style or defer to others. Leadership can also promote, and prevent, conflict.

HOW HAVE YOU RESOLVED GROUP CONFLICT?

When the word "conflict" is mentioned, what comes to mind? For many people, conflict is synonymous with fighting or negativity. However, conflict is not necessarily negative; some conflict is healthy for groups because it means there is a diversity of ideas and an emotional investment in the group's outcomes. What are some positive outcomes of conflict?

Conflict can be positive for groups if it helps them work through differences and encourages the input of all group members. This often happens during the storming phase we defined earlier. Conflict can also help prevent groupthink because it helps group members resist the urge to go along with ideas just to preserve cohesiveness.

Whether conflict is productive or destructive depends a great deal on the type of conflict and how a group manages it. In this context, we define **conflict** as "the process that occurs when group members, due to their interdependence, their real and perceived differences, and their emotions, engage in an expressed struggle that impedes task accomplishment" (Myers & Anderson, 2008, p. 203). Interdependence is important for conflict, because if group members do not need each other, there is no need for conflict. Task-oriented groups often face three different types of conflict.

Types of Group Conflict

Although there are a number of different types of group conflict to explore, we address how affective, ideational, and procedural impact our group experiences:

- **Affective conflict:** This type of conflict is rooted in interpersonal relationships, emotions, and personality differences. Note that "affective" conflict is not the same thing as "effective" conflict. Affective conflict is characterized by high emotional involvement. As an example, imagine that you are in a class group with someone that you do not like based on previous interactions or first impressions. You may bring those emotions into the group and contribute to affective conflict. This is the hardest type of conflict to resolve.
- **Ideational conflict:** In ideational conflict, group members have different opinions about problems. Unlike affective conflict, ideational conflict is not necessarily personal. An example is a disagreement about what the group will do for a presentation; one group member wants to do a skit and another group member thinks a formal slide show is appropriate. Or perhaps the group agrees to do an informative presentation on drug laws in the United States, but one member wants to present on the decriminalization of marijuana and another wants to present on prescription drug trafficking. Each group member may have a personal angle or interest, but the conflict is ultimately over ideas. However, this type of conflict can become affective conflict if it is not appropriately managed.
- **Procedural conflict:** This type of conflict involves differences of opinion about what procedures to use during group discussion and how to get the work done. For example, group members may disagree on whether the group should use majority vote or consensus for decision making. Group members may also disagree on a timeline for completing the work or on how responsibilities should be distributed; some may want to complete the work as soon as possible, whereas others may prefer to pull it together the week before the project is due. Procedural conflict happens when there is no framework for moving ahead. Setting shared goals early on and discussing how work will be completed can prevent some procedural conflict.

Conflict Management Styles

How do you handle conflict? Do you charge into it? Do you run away? Most people have a preferred way of managing conflict, although it can depend on what kind of

64 Chapter 4 Small Group Communication

conflict is occurring and an individual's relationship to a group. Thomas and Kilmann (1974) developed a measure to understand how people approached conflict differently. Conflict management styles are based on the degree to which you want to satisfy your own interests (*assertiveness*) and the degree to which you want to cooperate and satisfy the interests of others (*cooperation*) (Figure 4.3). Based on these two dimensions, there are five general conflict management styles. Each of these styles can be appropriate in different situations.

- **Avoiding style:** This style is low in assertiveness and cooperation. In avoiding, you are not concerned with satisfying either your interests or others' interests. This style is characterized by verbally and/or physically withdrawing from communication. Your goal is to change the topic quickly and to avoid a potential conflict.
- **Distributive styles:** This category includes both *competing* (high assertiveness, low cooperation) and *accommodating* (low assertiveness, high cooperation) styles. Distributive styles treat conflict as a sort of allotment of goods: one for me, none for you (or none for me, all for you). They are a win/lose approach; if one person wins, the other person loses.
- **Collaborating/integrative style:** This style includes high assertiveness and high cooperation; it is the style many of us claim we use most often. Collaboration results in a win-win situation because both sides have their needs met by looking for ways to combine their needs together. However, this can be time consuming and may not always be possible.
- **Compromising style:** This style is in between distributive and integrative styles. Both parties give up some of what they want to obtain part of what they want. Compromise can be problematic because it offers incomplete satisfaction for all parties. This can work well if it is a temporary solution, but it tends to not hold up in the long term.

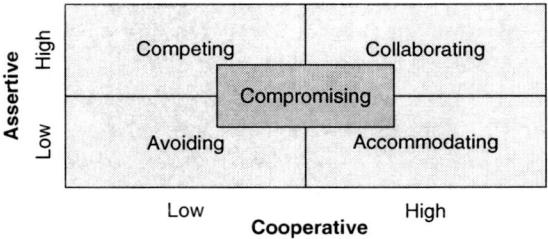

Figure 4.3 Thomas-Kilmann Conflict modes (image from creducation.org).
This diagram shows how conflict management styles are based on the degree to which you want to satisfy your own interests (assertiveness) and the degree to which you want to cooperate and satisfy the interests of others (cooperation).

The difference between collaboration and compromise can be difficult to understand. Take the example of a family vacation; you want to go to the beach, but your brother wants to go to an amusement park. Compromise would include going to the beach this year, and then the amusement park next year. You may be happy, but your brother will not be; next year your brother will be happy, but you may not be.

In contrast, collaboration means both interests can be met at the same time; an amusement park near the beach would allow you and your brother to have what you both want. The key to collaboration is to find out what appeals to the other person about their option, and what appeals to you about yours. If the beach itself is not as important as is the sun and warm weather, and if your brother is really looking for activities to stay busy, you might be able to find a different option that meets both of your needs (such as a cruise).

More important, the collaborative style of conflict management is not necessarily best. Avoiding may be very useful when the conflict is heated and parties need a "cooling off" period. The competing style may be used when an individual has special knowledge or expertise about the problem that the group is addressing, and when an individual is accountable for the consequences of the decision.

Think about your preferred style for conflict mediation. Discuss the benefits and drawbacks to your style with a good friend. Inquire how he or she responds to you when you use this style. This reflection is your way of analyzing small group communication climates. If your group has a defensive climate, you may find that conflicts are frequent and personal. However, conflict can also be an opportunity to change the climate of the group to a more supportive one.

HOW DO LISTENING, LANGUAGE, AND NONVERBAL BEHAVIORS WORK TOGETHER IN SMALL GROUP COMMUNICATION?

When you encounter group conflict, consider using the skills learned in previous chapters to manage the conflict effectively. First, *listen* to all perspectives in the conflict, even the perspectives of those members who may not be directly involved. Conflict may affect each person's participation in the group whether or not it involves them directly. After arriving at the choice to listen to another person (moving past listening selectively), try to avoid interrupting by *withholding judgment*. Even though doing so may be difficult because tensions are high, when you avoid prejudging or rehearsing a response before the person has finished speaking, you are demonstrating your ethics of listening in small group communication.

Similarly, *language behaviors* such as *paraphrasing* help you clarify, thereby checking your comprehension (e.g., "What I hear you saying is . . ."). You can *reframe* the disagreement and remember that "we" language creates less defensiveness than does "you" language. Focus on *description* and *problem orientation* rather than on evaluation and control. Maintaining a supportive climate does not mean that you must follow an accommodating style, where you give in to the wants of others. Using effective *listening behaviors,* such as *focusing your attention* and *attending to main points,* and not to the group members as individuals, can be beneficial to finding a satisfactory outcome for all.

Furthermore, consider how technology factors into group conflict. Group members can have varying motivations, knowledge, and skills, and their differences can reverberate. Sometimes we assume that all college students are proficient with technology, but that is not so (Ito, 2010). Have you worked in a group where only one or two people knew how to use the software? Have you relied on technology only to have problems with file sharing or compatibility? Have you tried to meet group members online only to have the Wi-Fi fail? Have you had group members use technology as an excuse for social loafing? Have you used that excuse yourself? If you have, than you should be able to see how technology can contribute to *affective, ideational,* and *procedural* conflict.

The enactment of group roles can also affect conflict. We easily identify ego-centered roles as catalysts for conflict, but the balance of group roles also affect conflict and how groups might resolve it. Consider a group with two *initiators* and two *encouragers:* the group could run into *ideational* conflict because they can generate many ideas, but may not be able to adequately think through the ideas without an *elaborator* or an *information giver/seeker.* Similarly, a *dominator* in a group of followers may not create much conflict, but this combination of roles tends not to lead to the best decisions.

Conclusion

In this chapter, we explored the key characteristics of size, interdependence, and identity that define small groups. We described the four phases of development that small groups experience. In addition to learning the practical skills for leading group meetings through agendas and taking minutes, we discovered how small group communication is unique in the balance of task and relational communication and group roles. We also considered the skills and techniques that groups need to make effective decisions, and styles of group leadership.

Finally, we identified three types of conflict (affective, ideational, and procedural) and five styles for managing group conflict (avoiding, competing, accommodating, collaborating, and compromising). We discussed ways in which listening and nonverbal cues work together in small group communication. Ultimately, we found that these interrelated concepts help develop the competence needed to communicate effectively and appropriately in small group contexts.

REFERENCES

Barge, J. K. 1997. Leadership as communication. In *Managing group life: communicating in decision-making groups,* ed. L. R. Frey and J. K. Barge, 202–233. New York: Houghton Mifflin.

Benne, K. D., and Sheats, P. 2007. Functional roles of group members. *Group Facilitation* 8:30–5. (Reprinted from *Journal of Social Issues* 4:41–9, 1948.)

Conklin, T. A. 2009. Creating classrooms of preference: an exercise in appreciative inquiry. *Journal of Management Education* 33:772–92. DOI:10.1177/1052562909333888

Cooperrider, D. L., Whitney, D., and Stavros, J. M. 2008. *Appreciative inquiry handbook: for leaders of change*. 2nd ed. Bedford Heights, OH: Lakeshore.

Di Salvo, V. S., Nikkel, E., and Monroe, C. 1989. A field investigation and identification of group members' perceptions of problems facing natural work groups. *Small Group Research* 20:551–67. DOI:10.1177/104649648902000411

Freeman, K. A. 1996. Attitudes toward work in project groups as predictors of group performance. *Small Group Research* 27:265–82. DOI:10.1177/1046496496272004

Gouran, D. S. 1999. Communication in groups: the emergence and evolution of a field of study. In *The handbook of group communication theory and research*, ed. L. R. Frey, D. S. Gouran, and M. S. Poole, 3–36. Thousand Oaks, CA: Sage.

Hollander, E. P. 1978. *Leadership dynamics: a practical guide to effective relationships*. New York: Free Press.

Ito, M. 2010. *Hanging out, messing around, and geeking out*. Boston, MA: The MIT Press.

Janis, I. 1972. *Victims of groupthink: a psychological study of foreign-policy decisions and fiascoes*. Boston, MA: Houghton Mifflin.

Janis, I. 1982. *Groupthink: psychological studies of policy decisions and fiascos*. 2nd ed. Boston, MA: Houghton Mifflin.

Keyton, J. 2006. *Communicating in groups: building relationships for group effectiveness*. 3rd ed. New York: Oxford University Press.

Keyton, J. 1999. Relational communication in groups. In *The handbook of group communication theory and research*, ed. L. R. Frey, D. S. Gouran, and M. S. Poole, 192–222. Thousand Oaks, CA: Sage.

Keyton, J., and Frey, L. R. 2002. The state of traits: predispositions and group communication. In *New directions in group communication*, ed. L. R. Frey, 99–120. Thousand Oaks, CA: Sage.

Lahman, M. 2012. Appreciative inquiry: guided reflection to generate change in service-learning courses. *Communication Teacher* 26:1–4. DOI:10.1080/17404622.2011.625362

Latane, B., Williams, K., and Harkins, S. 1979. Many hands make light the work: the causes and consequences of social loafing. *Journal of Personality and Social Psychology* 37:822–32. DOI:10.1037/0022-3514.37.6.822

Lewin, K., Lippitt, R., and White, R. K. 1939. Patterns of aggressive behavior in experimentally created "social climates." *Journal of Social Psychology* 10:271–99. DOI:10.1080/00224545.1939.9713366

Morreale, S. P., Spitzberg, B. H., and Barge, J. K. 2007. *Human communication: motivation, knowledge, and skills.* 2nd ed. Belmont, CA: Thomson Wadsworth.

Myers, S. A., and Anderson. C. M. 2008. *The fundamentals of small group communication.* Thousand Oaks, CA: Sage.

Schawbel, D. 2012. *Millennial Branding student employment gap survey.* Retrieved from http://millennialbranding.com/2012/05/millennial-branding-student-employment-gap-study.

Socha, T. J. 1997. Group communication across the life span. In *Managing group life: communicating in decision making groups*, ed. L. R. Frey and J. K. Barge, 3–28. Boston, MA: Houghton Mifflin.

Thomas, K. W., and Kilmann, R. H. 1974. *The Thomas–Kilmann conflict mode instrument.* Tuxedo Park, NY: Xicom.

Tuckman, B. W. 1965. Developmental sequence in small groups. *Psychological Bulletin* 63(6):384–99. DOI:10.1037/h0022100

Wood, J. T., Phillips, G. M., and Pedersen, D. J. 1986. *Group discussion: a practical guide to participation and leadership.* 2nd ed. New York: Harper & Row.

GLOSSARY

accommodating style: a conflict management style characterized by low assertiveness and high cooperation.

ad hominem fallacy: a fallacy of irrelevance that occurs when the speaker attacks the character or actions of a person instead of addressing the argument the person is making.

ad populum: a fallacy of irrelevance that appeals to the popularity of something or someone.

agenda: a list of topics that need to be covered at a meeting.

affective conflict: conflict rooted in interpersonal relationships, emotions, and personality differences.

analogy: a comparison between two things based on similarities or resemblances between them.

appreciative inquiry: a method for organizational change that focuses on what is going well with a project and how to make it better.

appreciative listening: listening for enjoyment.

appropriate: when communication behavior follows the rules and norms of a context.

argumentum ad populum fallacy: also called the bandwagon fallacy, this fallacy makes an argument based on the popularity of something.

articulation: speaking words correctly and clearly.

artifacts: nonverbal communication that uses objects to communicate something about the person, such as clothing, cell phones, and body art.

attentiveness: the interpersonal skill of showing interest and concern to another person.

audience analysis: discovering information about your audience prior to developing a speech in order to make the topic relevant to the audience.

aural: related to hearing.

autocratic leadership: a directive leadership style where the leader takes on a guiding and instructive role.

avoiding style: a conflict management style that is low in assertiveness and cooperation—verbally and physically withdrawing from the conflict.

behavioral interdependence: a form of group interdependence where the verbal and nonverbal messages that members send affect other group members.

body movement: nonverbal using their body in space to communicate or emphasize a point, for example, walking around the room.

bypassing: the listener and speaker act as if the words mean the same thing to each person, but their interpretations are different.

channel: medium through which the message is sent.

clarifying questions: follow-up questions we ask a speaker to explore another's perspective.

collaborating/integrating style: a conflict management style characterized by both high assertiveness and high cooperation; the style tries to find the win-win outcome for both parties.

communication: the process of creating meaning together.

communication competence: the ability to choose behaviors that are appropriate and effective for the context.

communication competence grid: four quadrants designed to demonstrate varying degrees of communication competence (appropriate/effective, appropriate/ineffective, effective/inappropriate, inappropriate/ineffective).

competing style: a conflict management style characterized by high assertiveness and low cooperation.

composure: interpersonal skill of displaying assertiveness, confidence, and being in control.

comprehensive listening: listening for understanding.

compromising style: a conflict management style where both parties give up some of what they want to get part of what they want.

conclusion: the final part of the speech, which should reiterate the main points and close memorably.

conflict: when communicators disagree and see their goals as incompatible.

context: a situation, for example, public speaking, interpersonal, and small group contexts.

coordination: interpersonal skill of managing the timing, initiation, closure, and topics in an interaction.

critical advisor: a group member(s) who takes on a role of raising potential negative aspects of a group's decision.

critical listening: listening to evaluate.

culture: values and behaviors shared by a group.

decoding: the meaning the receiver interprets from the message.

deductive logic: when a claim or assertion is based on a generally accepted premise applied to a specific example.

defensive communication climates: negative communication environments.

democratic leadership: a leadership style that tries to get everyone involved in the decision- making process and to maintain positive relationships with all group members.

dependence: a group state were individuals are in a subordinate position to other group members or cannot work together without being in each other's presence.

distributive styles: includes both competing and accommodating conflict management styles; a win/lose approach to conflict.

effective: when communication behavior accomplishes a desired goal.

elaboration strategies: a listening strategy that involves expanding and explaining a message to enhance understanding.

empathetic listening: listening for feelings.

encoding: the meaning the sender puts in the message.

enthymeme: a truncated syllogism; an informal logic structure that requires the audience to fill in part of the argument.

environmental noise: anything in the context that might affect speaking and listening, such as air conditioning or heating fans, people talking, keyboards clicking, and music playing.

ethics: values in action.

ethos: the credibility and ethics of a speaker.

expressiveness: interpersonal skill of displaying vividness and animation in verbal and nonverbal expression.

extemporaneous speech: a planned but conversational speech delivered with notes.

extrovert: a person who enjoys multiple casual messages, likes to think out loud, replies promptly and prefers talking to listening.

eye contact: looking directly at another person or the audience.

facial expressions: nonverbal cues using the face to show mood or emotion, for example, smiling.

feedback: an indication from the receiver of how the message was interpreted.

gender-neutral language: language that does not privilege one gender over another; for example, using "humans" instead of "mankind."

gestures: movements of the hands and arms to emphasize points or communicate a message.

goal interdependence: members rely on each other to complete the task

grammar: the rules of correct speech in a language.

grouphate: a negative predisposition toward group work that causes people to dislike working in groups.

group identity: the psychological and/or physical boundaries that distinguish a group member from a non-group member.

group roles: informal and unassigned sets of behaviors that individuals perform; can be task, relational, or ego-centered.

groupthink: faulty group decision making resulting from an insulated and cohesive group that values consensus as the highest priority.

haptics: nonverbal communication that involves touch, which can communicate power, support, and intimacy.

hasty generalization fallacy: a generalization fallacy where a broad conclusion is made based on too little evidence to make the claim.

ideational conflict: conflict that occurs that when group members have different opinions about the problem.

inductive logic: drawing a conclusion based on a series of specific examples or instances.

information transfer model: a linear model of communication where senders and receivers send messages one at a time through a channel.

interdependence: a characteristic of small groups; any group member's behavior influences group members' task and relational behaviors.

introduction: the opening part of a speech that catches the audience's attention and includes a clear thesis statement and preview of main ideas.

introvert: a person who prefers to listen deeply to one message at a time, reflects before responding, and uses language precisely.

kinesics: nonverbal communication that uses the body, including movement, posture, gestures, facial expressions, and eye contact.

knowledge: understanding how to communicate—a component necessary to be a competent communicator.

language: symbols used to negotiate meaning.

laissez-faire leadership: a hands-off style of leadership where the group works independently and the leader steps in when requested.

listening: the process of receiving, constructing meaning from, and responding to spoken and/or nonverbal messages.

listening-centered approach: *an approach to communication where you seek first to understand the perspective of the other person.*

leadership: a communication process that helps groups organize themselves to meet desired goals.

logical fallacy: an intentional or unintentional error in logic that leads the listener to false conclusions.

logos: using sound reasoning and evidence to persuade.

manuscript speech: a speech that is written out word-for-word and then read to the audience.

maximizing: communication behavior that may be effective but is not appropriate.

Meaning: definitions found in people and contexts.

memorized speech: a speech that is fully written out, memorized, and then recited to the audience word-for-word.

message: content or information shared in the information transfer model; an action to which we attach meaning in the transactional model.

metaphor: a figure of speech that compares two things/people/events without the use of "like" or "as."

minimizing: communication behavior that is both inappropriate and ineffective.

minutes: a written record of the topics and decisions discussed during a meeting.

monochronic time: a culture-specific use of time that focuses on doing one thing at a time; followers of monochronic time value punctuality and efficiency.

motivation: the desire to communicate—a component necessary to be a competent communicator.

noise: environmental sounds, physiological distractions, and semantic interference that hinder the communication process.

nonverbal codes: cues that stand alone and/or accompany language.

norms: unspoken expectations of behavior.

optimizing: communication behavior that is both appropriate and effective.

paraphrasing: summarizing a speaker's content and feelings in your own words.

pathos: persuasive emotional appeals.

performative competence: the part of communication competence that we enact through behaviors.

persuasive speech: speaking with intent to influence an audience's attitudes, beliefs, values, or behaviors and moving listeners to change or to action.

physiological noise: any distraction that involves the body, such as hunger, fatigue, and illness.

polychronic time: a culture-specific approach to time where tasks overlap; followers of polychronic time are less schedule-driven and focus on relationships.

Post hoc fallacy: a cause-effect fallacy that presupposes that one event caused another event to happen.

presentational aids: sensory aids used during a speech, such as slides, a chart, a song clip, a video, or handouts.

procedural conflict: conflict about what procedures to use for group discussion or decision making or how the work gets done.

process competence: the cognitive knowledge that allows individuals to communicate competently.

proxemics: a category of nonverbal communication involving the use of space, such as personal distance or spatial arrangement.

receiver: the decoder of message.

reference: what comes to mind to connect the symbol and the referent in the triangle of meaning.

referent: the thing or idea to which the symbol refers in the triangle of meaning.

reframing: finding a new angle from which to view a topic and speaker.

repetition: emphasizing a main idea by repeating it during a speech to help the audience remember.

relational communication: group messages that build connections and relationships and establish the climate of the group.

rhetoric: according to Aristotle, the ability to use the available and appropriate means of persuasion in any given situation.

rhetorical canons: Aristotle's five essential activities for persuasive speaking: invention, arrangement, style, memory, and delivery.

salience: in the context of speech preparation, the importance of a topic to your audience.

semantic noise: interference caused by not knowing the meaning of a word.

sender: the originator of a message.

shared field of meaning: understanding of another person's experiences, values, attitudes, and beliefs.

simile: a figure of speech that compares two things/people/events using "like" or "as."

situational analysis: consideration of aspects of the speaking situation prior to giving a speech, including time of day and environmental factors such as the speaking space

skills: demonstrating effective and appropriate behaviors—a component necessary to be a competent communicator.

slippery slope fallacy: a cause-effect fallacy that suggests that one event automatically leads to a series of other undesirable events.

small group: three or more people working interdependently for the purpose of accomplishing a task.

social loafing: a behavior where individual efforts decrease because the group is too large or the task or the contributions are not perceived as valuable.

source: see sender.

standard agenda: a systematic process for decision making based on the functional theory of decision making.

sufficing: appropriate communication behavior that is not effective.

supportive communication climates: positive communication environments.

sweeping generalization fallacy: a generalization fallacy that clusters ideas, people, or objects into one group and implies that all the items in the group are the same.

syllogism: a deductive logic structure consisting of a generally accepted major premise, a specific minor premise, and a conclusion.

symbol: the word which refers to a referent in the triangle of meaning.

task communication: messages based on the group objectives and activities.

tone: the quality of a voice that can express meaning or emotion.

transactional model of communication: model of communication that stresses the simultaneity of the communication interaction and how we interact through a shared field of meaning.

transitions: words and phrases that connect main ideas and support material within a speech. Transitions serve as guideposts to let the listener know when you are moving on to another idea.

vocalics: also called paralanguage, nonverbal communication that uses the voice, including rate, pitch, and volume.

volume: the loudness/softness or intensity of a speaker's voice.

CPSIA information can be obtained
at www.ICGtesting.com
Printed in the USA
FFOW01n2034140717
37818FF